The Reference Shelf™

Intellectual Property

Edited by Jennifer Peloso

The Reference Shelf
Volume 75 • Number 5

The H. W. Wilson Company
2003

The Reference Shelf

The books in this series contain reprints of articles, excerpts from books, addresses on current issues, and studies of social trends in the United States and other countries. There are six separately bound numbers in each volume, all of which are usually published in the same calendar year. Numbers one through five are each devoted to a single subject, providing background information and discussion from various points of view and concluding with a subject index and comprehensive bibliography that lists books, pamphlets, and abstracts of additional articles on the subject. The final number of each volume is a collection of recent speeches, and it contains a cumulative speaker index. Books in the series may be purchased individually or on subscription.

Library of Congress has cataloged this title as follows:

Intellectual property / edited by Jennifer Peloso.
p. cm. — (The reference shelf; v. 75, no. 5)
Includes bibliographical references and index.
ISBN 0-8242-1023-9 (alk. paper)
1. Intellectual property—United States. I. Peloso, Jennifer. II. Series.

KF2979.I415 2003
346.7304'8—dc22

2003059282

Cover: Business Concept, by Geoff Brightling (© Taxi/Getty Images).

Visit H.W. Wilson's Web site: www.hwwilson.com

Printed in the United States of America

Contents

Preface

As the world becomes more technologically advanced, greater access is available to other people's ideas. It is this access that has necessitated greater protection of intellectual property, and the laws governing this protection have become more controversial. Intellectual property is defined by *Encarta World English Dictionary* as "property from original thought protected by law: original creative work manifested in a tangible form that can be legally protected, for example, by a patent, trademark, or copyright." The protection of intellectual property is at the heart of a heated debate. Though it is important to have access to information, it is also important to respect creators' rights to the materials they produce. Since the Internet has become such a huge information outlet, the regulation of information passed along the Internet has become a central issue in protecting intellectual property—especially as hackers find more and more ways to download, swap, and burn multimedia works, and then pass those techniques onto others.

Congress is caught in the middle of this debate and is trying to come to terms with how to handle the protection of intellectual property while not restricting the dissemination of ideas. The controversy stems from the fact that both sides—the creators and those who seek to use their products—make some valid points. On the one hand, there are fair-use advocates who believe that without access to information, or the legal means to use that information, science, medicine, and almost every other aspect of academia would be stifled, and new ideas, inventions, and medicines would never be possible. On the other hand, those with a more conservative view think that people have the right to protect their ideas and words and deserve the credit for them that a copyright conveys. Although both of these arguments are reasonable, the question is, where do you draw the line? How do you protect the rights of scientists, inventors, and writers while making enough information about their work available to the public so that others may benefit from these new ideas and innovations?

This book considers these issues while exploring the world of intellectual property. It also deals with the debate surrounding the safeguarding of intellectual property, how people are affected by IP laws, and what is being done to protect ideas spread through various forms of media.

As its title suggests, Chapter 1, "What Is Intellectual Property?" is an overview of the topic at hand. It describes what intellectual property is, who owns ideas, how to distinguish between copyrights, trademarks, and patents, and the pros and cons of protecting intellectual property in today's high-tech world.

Chapter 2 examines the problem of plagiarism, a serious breach of law and ethics whether committed with or without intention. While examining specific instances of plagiarism that have recently rocked the publishing world—such as the Jayson Blair scandal at the *New York Times*—this chapter also discusses plagiarism in high schools and colleges, how to detect plagiarism, and how to avoid stealing someone else's ideas.

The focus of Chapter 3 is on copyrights. Along with considering what a copyright is, this chapter looks at how writers' work is being spread over the Internet without their knowledge or monetary compensation and examines the most recent laws passed extending copyrights, such as the Digital Millennium Copyright Act. It also discusses several highly publicized court cases that have been at the center of the copyright debate—including *United States v. ElcomSoft Ltd.* (a case of international copyright infringement) and *Tasini et al. v. The New York Times et al.* (an example of the frustration many writers are feeling due to copyright laws).

The final chapter, "21st-Century Piracy," considers a problem that has plagued digital media. It begins by looking at one of the most high-profile cases of piracy—the dispute against Napster and its fallout. The chapter continues by examining several important issues, including international piracy and how other countries infringe on American copyright laws; the pirating of DVDs; and the illegal broadcast of TV programs via the Web.

I would like to thank all the authors and publishers who granted us permission to reprint their work. I would also especially like to thank Lynn Messina, Sandra Watson, Gray Young, Rich Stein, and Norris Smith for all of their help, guidance, and patience; without them, this book would not have been possible.

Jennifer Peloso
October 2003

I. What Is Intellectual Property?

Editor's Introduction

At the start of the 21st century, while the world is still plagued by the usual culprits—drugs, crime, war, and so on—an increasing number of today's courtroom battles are being waged over a new problem: intellectual property protection. Ideas, words, thoughts, and designs—more specifically, the *protection* of them—are what people seem to be fighting over these days. Disputes involving these forms of intellectual property (IP) have split individuals into two camps. Some are in favor of anti-piracy measures and strict protection of IP, while others want easy access to material they feel would benefit society at large. Before one can protect intellectual property, however, one must understand what intellectual property is and why the debate over it is so heated. Chapter 1, "What Is Intellectual Property?," provides an overview of this subject.

The chapter begins with "Creation Myths," an article by Douglas Clement that compares and contrasts the two sides of the intellectual property protection debate by asking whether IP protection is too strict and stifling the growth of new ideas. In Douglas Clement's discussion, two economists, Michele Boldrin and David K. Levine, represent the side which believes that America has gone overboard in its efforts to protect intellectual property. Intermingled throughout are the opinions of those who represent the other side and challenge Boldrin and Levine's ideas as flawed arguments.

Many times the split over protecting intellectual property is between those who own intellectual property and those who want to use it. Today, many companies, newspapers, and magazines hire independent contractors or freelancers to do work for them, but the freelancers have no idea that what they just created belongs not to them but to the one who hired them. It is important for creators to know who will own the rights to their products before they create them. Understanding from the beginning who owns different types of intellectual property is therefore very important in the discussion of protecting IP—not only to protect the rights of the creator, but also to save the cost of legal fees later on. "Avoiding Intellectual Property Disputes" by Lien Verbauwhede addresses these concerns in regard to inventions, copyrights, and industrial designs. Verbauwhede discusses the differences between IP created by employees and that created by independent contractors and explains how the law dictates ownership rights in these two situations. A sidebar offers practical advice on how to avoid conflicts in these areas.

It is also very important to know where the government stands on the intellectual property debate. Are lawmakers in favor of fair use, in which people may use copyrighted materials without going through the formality of obtaining permission, or do they lean more towards strict protection? In "Fair Use and Abuse," Gary Stix compares different legislative bills designed to protect intellectual property. From the hard-line Consumer Broadband and Digital Television Promotion Act—which looks to solidify already existing anti-piracy measures—to more lenient bills which try to promote fair use as long as it does not infringe on copyrights, this article explores the different ways government officials are trying to protect or thwart the public's attempt to use others' IP. An accompanying sidebar from the Copyright Office of the Library of Congress lists factors for helping one determine whether "fair use" is plausible in certain situations, as well as past uses of works that the courts have deemed legal under "fair use" standards.

Similar to "fair use" is the idea of "open-source." Both are based on the principle of limited IP protection and of publicly sharing and accessing works, ideas, and information in order to benefit society at large. They differ in that open-source refers primarily to software, rather than written works. In his article "Open-Source Software Development," Georg von Krogh discusses an agreement among software developers to share ideas and designs in an open forum in the hope of benefitting from the diverse mix of expertise imparted. Von Krogh also gives a brief history of this new phenomenon of IP sharing and describes its benefits, the process behind it, and a future where open-source software is widespread.

Paul Andrews attempts to answer the question, Is open-source the next wave of the future? in his article "Attack of the Freebie Software." Andrews takes a look at how big-name companies, along with corporations, schools, and even governments, are switching from Microsoft to Linux servers, which offer open-source software. As this battle between Microsoft and Linux intensifies, Andrews examines the pros and cons of each, how each is affecting the other's business, the reasons behind the switch to Linux, and the cost incentives that either promote and/or discourage its use.

While it helps to know what the government is doing to protect IP rights, one must also know how to protect one's own rights through, for instance, patents, trademarks, and copyrights. In "Protections on Intellectual Properties Do Differ," Maxine Lans Retsky examines these three safeguards to IP. She looks at what they are designed to protect, the similarities and differences among them, how they can be obtained, how long they last, and how much each costs.

The final article in this chapter, "Drug Companies Battle in the War over Generics" by Glenn Singer, examines the dilemma over drug patents. With prescription drug costs on the rise, patients are looking for ways to alleviate the high expense of medications. The answer is generic drugs, but patent protections and renewals are preventing many generic drugs from entering the market. Singer looks at the problem of medicinal patents and the benefits to society if generic drugs were more easily marketed.

Creation Myths[1]

BY DOUGLAS CLEMENT
REASON, MARCH 2003

The most forceful performance at last year's Grammy ceremony was a speech by Michael Greene, then president of the National Academy of Recording Arts and Sciences. Speaking not long after the 9/11 attacks, Greene gravely warned of a worldwide threat—"pervasive, out of control, and oh so criminal"—and implored his audience to "embrace this life-and-death issue."

Greene was not referring to international terrorism. "The most insidious virus in our midst," he said sternly, "is the illegal downloading of music on the Net."

Greene's sermon may have been a bit overwrought, but he's not alone in his fears. During the last decade, the captains of many industries—music, movies, publishing, software, pharmaceuticals—have railed against the "piracy" of their profits. Copyright and patent protections have been breached by new technologies that quickly copy and distribute their products to mass markets. And as quickly as a producer figures a way to encrypt a DVD or software program to prevent duplication, some hacker in Seattle, Reykjavik, or Manila figures a way around it.

The music industry has tried to squelch the threat, most conspicuously by suing Napster, the wildly popular Internet service that matched patrons with the songs they wanted, allowing them to download digital music files without charge. Napster lost the lawsuit and was liquidated, while similar services survive.

But the struggle over Napster-like services has accented a much broader issue: How does an economy best promote innovation? Do patents and copyrights nurture or stifle it? Have we gone too far in protecting intellectual property?

In a paper that has gained wide attention (and caught serious flak) for challenging the conventional wisdom, economists Michele Boldrin and David K. Levine answer the final question with a resounding *yes*. Copyrights, patents, and similar government-granted rights serve only to reinforce monopoly control, with its attendant damages of inefficiently high prices, low quantities, and stifled future innovation, they write in "Perfectly Competitive Innovation," a report published by the Federal Reserve Bank of Minneapolis. More to the point, they argue, economic theory shows

1. Article by Douglas Clement from *Reason* March 2003. Copyright © *Reason*. Reprinted with permission.

that perfectly competitive markets are entirely capable of rewarding (and thereby stimulating) innovation, making copyrights and patents superfluous and wasteful.

Free markets might fail to bring about optimal levels of innovation.

Reactions to the paper have been mixed. Robert Solow, the MIT economist who won a Nobel Prize in 1987 for his work on growth theory, wrote Boldrin and Levine a letter calling the paper "an eye-opener" and making suggestions for further refinements. Danny Quah of the London School of Economics calls their analysis "an important and profound development" that "seeks to overturn nearly half a century of formal economic thinking on intellectual property." But UCLA economist Benjamin Klein finds their work "unrealistic," and Paul Romer, a Stanford economist whose path-breaking development of new growth theory is the focus of much of Boldrin and Levine's critique, considers their logic flawed and their assumptions implausible.

"We're not claiming to have invented anything new, really," says Boldrin. "We're recognizing something that we think has been around ever since there has been innovation. In fact, patents and copyrights are a very recent distortion." Even so, they're working against a well-established conventional wisdom that has sanctioned if not embraced intellectual property rights, and theirs is a decidedly uphill battle.

The Conventional Wisdom

In the 1950s Solow showed that technological change was a primary source of economic growth, but his models treated that change as a given determined by elements beyond pure economic forces. In the 1960s Kenneth Arrow, Karl Shell, and William Nordhaus analyzed the relationship between markets and technological change. They concluded that free markets might fail to bring about optimal levels of innovation.

In a landmark 1962 article, Arrow gave three reasons why perfect competition might fail to allocate resources optimally in the case of invention. "We expect a free enterprise economy to underinvest in invention and research (as compared with an ideal)," he wrote, "because it is risky, because the product can be appropriated only to a limited extent, and because of increasing returns in use."

Risk does seem a clear roadblock to investment in technological change. Will all the hours and dollars spent on research and development result in a profitable product? Is the payoff worth the risk? The uncertainty of success diminishes the desire to try. Much of Arrow's article examines economic means of dealing with uncertainty, none of them completely successful.

The second problem, what economists call inappropriability, is the divergence between social and private benefit—in this case, the difference between the benefit society would reap from an invention and the benefit reaped by the inventor. Will I try to invent the wheel if all humanity would benefit immeasurably from my invention but I'd get only $1,000? Maybe not. Property rights, well-defined, help address the issue.

The third obstacle is indivisibility. The problem here is that the act of invention involves a substantial upfront expenditure (of time or money) before a single unit of the song, formula, or book exists. But thereafter, copies can be made at a fraction of the cost. Such indivisibilities result in dramatically increasing returns to scale: If a $1 million investment in research and development results in just one unit of an invention, the prototype, a $2 million expenditure could result in the prototype plus thousands or millions of duplicates.

This is a great problem to have, but perfect competition doesn't deal well with increasing returns to scale. With free markets and no barriers to entry, products are priced at their marginal cost (that is, the cost of the latest copy), and that price simply won't cover the huge initial outlay—that is, the large indivisibility that is necessary to create the prototype. Inventors will have no financial incentive for bringing their inventions to reality, and society will be denied the benefits.

Increasing returns therefore seem to argue for some form of monopoly, and in the late 1970s Joseph Stiglitz and Avinash Dixit developed a growth model of monopolistic competition—that is, limited competition with increasing returns to scale. It's a model in which many firms compete in a given market but none is strictly a price taker. (In other words, each has some ability to restrict output and raise prices, like a monopolist.) It's a growth model, in other words, without perfect competition. The Dixit-Stiglitz model is widely used today, with the underlying assumption that economic growth requires technological change, which implies increasing returns, which means imperfect competition.

Stanford's Paul Romer formalized much of this work in the 1980s and 1990s, in what he called a theory of endogenous growth. The idea was that technological change—innovation—should be modeled as part of an economy, not outside it as Solow had done. The policy implication was that economic variables, such as interest and tax rates, as well as subsidies for research and technical education, could influence the rate of innovation.

Romer refined the ideas of Arrow and others, developing new terms, integrating the economics of innovation and extending the Dixit-Stiglitz growth model into what he called "new growth theory." In a parallel track, Robert Lucas, a Nobel laureate at the University of Chicago, elucidated the importance of human capital to economic growth. And just prior to all this growth theory work, Paul Krugman, Elhanan Helpman, and others integrated increasing returns theory with international trade economics, creating "new trade theory." Similar theories became the bedrock of industrial organization economics.

Central to Romer's theory is the idea of nonrivalry, a property he considers inherent to invention, designs, and other forms of intellectual creation. "A purely nonrival good," he wrote, "has the property that its use by one firm or person in no way limits its use by another." A formula, for example, can be used simultaneously and equally by 100 people, whereas a wrench cannot.

Nonrivalrous goods are inherently subject to increasing returns to scale, says Romer. "Developing new and better instructions is equivalent to incurring a fixed cost," he wrote. "Once the cost of creating a new set of instructions has been incurred, the instructions can be used over and over again at no additional cost." But if this is true, then "it follows directly that an equilibrium with price taking cannot be supported." In other words, economic growth—and the technological innovation it requires—aren't possible under perfect competition; they require some degree of monopoly power.

Economic growth—and the technological innovation it requires—aren't possible under perfect competition; they require some degree of monopoly power.

Undermining Convention

Economists prize economic growth but distrust monopoly, so accepting the latter to obtain the former is a Faustian bargain at best. With "Perfectly Competitive Innovation," Boldrin and Levine vigorously reject the contract.

Innovation, they argue, has occurred in the past without substantial protection of intellectual property. "Historically, people have been inventing and writing books and music when copyright did not exist," notes Boldrin. "Mozart wrote a lot of very beautiful things without any copyright protection." (The publishers of music and books, on the other hand, sometimes did have copyrights in the materials they bought from their creators.)

Contemporary examples are also plentiful. The fashion world—highly competitive, with designs largely unprotected—innovates constantly and profitably. A Gucci is a Gucci; knock-offs are mere imitations and worth less than the original, so Gucci—for better or worse—still has an incentive to create. The financial securities industry makes millions by developing and selling complex securities and options without benefit of intellectual property protection. Competitors are free to copy a firm's security package, but doing so takes time. The initial developer's first-mover advantage secures enough profit to justify "inventing" the security.

As for software, Boldrin refers to an MIT working paper by economists Eric Maskin and James Bessen. Maskin and Bessen write that "some of the most innovative industries today—software, computers and semiconductors—have historically had weak patent protection and have experienced rapid imitation of their products."

Moreover, U.S. court decisions in the 1980s that strengthened patent protection for software led to less innovation. "Far from unleashing a flurry of new innovative activity," Maskin and Bessen write, "these stronger property rights ushered in a period of stagnant, if not declining, R&D among those industries and firms that patented most." Industries that depend on sequential product development—the initial version is followed by an improved second version, etc.—are, they argue, likely to be stifled by stronger intellectual property regimes.

"So examples abound," says Boldrin. "That's the empirical point: Evidence shows that innovators have enough of an incentive to innovate." But he and Levine are not, by nature or training, empiricists. They build mathematical models to describe economic theory. In the case of intellectual property, they contend, current theory says innovation won't happen unless innovators receive monopoly rights, but the evidence says otherwise. "So what we do is to develop the theoretical point to explain the evidence," says Boldrin.

***"Only ideas embodied in people, machines or goods have economic value."*—Michele Boldrin and David K. Levine, economists**

Rivalry Over Nonrivalry

A fundamental tenet of current conventional wisdom is that knowledge-based innovations are subject to increasing returns because ideas are nonrivalrous. Boldrin and Levine argue that in an economy this has no relevance. While pure ideas can be shared without rivalry in theory, the economic application of ideas is inherently rivalrous, because ideas "have economic value only to the extent that they are embodied into either something or someone." What is relevant in the economic realm is not an abstract concept or formula—no matter how beautiful—but its physical embodiment. Calculus is economically valuable only insofar as engineers and economists know and apply it. "Only ideas embodied in people, machines or goods have economic value," they write. And because of their physical embodiment, "valuable ideas . . . are as rivalrous as commodities containing no ideas at all, if such exist."

A novel is valuable only to the extent that it is written down (if then). A song can be sold only if it is sung, played, or printed by its creator. A software program—once written—might seem costless,

Boldrin and Levine write, but "the prototype does not sit on thin air. To be used by others it needs to be copied, which requires resources of various kinds, including time. To be usable it needs to reside on some portion of the memory of your computer. . . . When you are using that specific copy of the software, other people cannot simultaneously do the same."

In each instance, the development of the initial prototype is far more costly than the production of all subsequent copies. But because copying takes time—a limited commodity—and materials (paper, ink, disk space), it is not entirely costless. "Consider the paradigmatic example of the wheel," they write. "Once the first wheel was produced, imitation could take place at a cost orders of magnitude smaller. But even imitation cannot generate free goods: to make a new wheel, one needs to spend some time looking at the first one and learning how to carve it."

Development is one production process involving long hours, gallons of coffee, sweaty genius, and black, tempestuous moods.

The first wheel is far more valuable than all others, of course, but that "does not imply that the wheel, first or last that it be, is a nonrivalrous good. It only implies that, for some goods, replication costs are very small."

Economic theorists generally have assumed that the dramatic difference between development and replication costs can be modeled as a single process with increasing returns to scale: a huge fixed cost (the initial investment) followed by costless duplication. Boldrin and Levine say this misrepresents reality: There are two distinct processes with very different technologies. Development is one production process involving long hours, gallons of coffee, sweaty genius, and black, tempestuous moods. At the end of this initial process, the prototype (with any luck) exists and the effort and money that produced it are a sunk cost, an expense in the past.

Thereafter, a very different production process governs: Replicators study the original, gather flat stones, round off corners, bore center holes, and prune tree limbs into axles. Stone wheels roll off the antediluvian assembly line. In this second process, the economics of production are the same as for any other commodity, usually with constant returns to scale.

As Boldrin and Levine develop their mathematical model, they assume only that, "as in reality," copying takes time and there is a limit (less than infinity) on the number of copies that can be produced per unit of time. These "twin assumptions" introduce a slim element of rivalry. After it's created, the prototype can be either consumed or used for copying in the initial time period. (Technically, it could be used for both, but not as easily as if it were used for just one or the other.)

While others simply have assumed, with Romer, that the prototype of an intellectual product is nonrivalrous, Boldrin and Levine argue that the tiny cost of replicating it undermines the conventional model. Production is not subject to increasing returns, they argue, and competitive markets can work. "Even a minuscule amount of rivalry," they write, "can turn standard results upside down."

Britney Gets Her Due

Still, the central question is whether innovators will have enough incentive to go through the arduous, expensive invention process. Since the 1400s, when the first patent systems emerged in Venice, governments have tried to provide incentive by granting inventors sole rights to their creations for limited periods. The U.S. Constitution gives Congress the power "to promote the Progress of Science and useful Arts, by securing for limited Times to Authors and Inventors the exclusive Right to their respective Writings and Discoveries."

Economists long have recognized that such exclusive rights give creators monopolies, allowing them to set prices and quantities that may not be socially optimal. But conventional thinking says these costs are the necessary tradeoff for bringing forth creative genius. Today, the legal realities and economic conventions have assumed the air of incontrovertible fact: If inventors can be "ripped off"—copied as soon as they create—why would they bother?

In arguing for competitive innovation rather than the monopolistic variety, Boldrin and Levine emphasize that they are not saying creators don't have rights. On the contrary, they stress that innovators should be given "a well defined right of first sale." (Or, more technically, "we assume full appropriability of privately produced commodities.") And creators should be paid the full market value of their invention, the first unit of the new product. That value is "the net discounted value of the future stream of consumption services" generated by that first unit, which is an economist's way of saying it's worth the current value of everything it's going to earn in the future.

So if Britney Spears records a new song, she should be able to sell the initial recording for the sum total of whatever music distributors think her fans will pay for copies of the music during the next century or so. Distributors know her songs are in demand, and she knows she can command a high price. As in any other market, the buyer and seller negotiate a deal. The same rules would hold for a novelist who writes a book, a software programmer who generates code, or a physicist who develops a useful formula. They get to sell the invention in a competitive market. They're paid whatever the market will bear, and if the market values copies of their song, book, code, or formula, the initial prototype will be precious and they'll be well paid.

In fact, says Boldrin, "in a competitive market, the very first few copies are very valuable because those are the instruments which the imitators—the other people who will publish your stuff—will use to make copies. They're more capital goods than consumption goods. So the initial copies will be sold at a very high price, but then very rapidly they will go down in price."

What creators won't get, in Boldrin and Levine's world, is the right to impose downstream licensing agreements that prevent customers from reproducing the product, modifying it, or using it as a stepping stone to the next innovation. They can't prevent their customers from competing with them.

But will the market pay the creator enough? That depends on the innovator's opportunity costs. If the price likely to be paid for an invention's first sale exceeds the opportunity costs of the inventor, then yes, the inventor will create. If a writer spends a year on a book, and could have earned $30,000 during that year doing something else, then her opportunity cost is $30,000. Only if she guesses she can sell her book for at least that much is she likely to sit down and write.

Monopoly rights are not only unnecessary for innovation but may stifle it.

"What we show in the technical paper is that the amount [a book publisher] gives me is positive, and in fact, it can be large," says Boldrin. "Then it's up to me to figure out if what society is paying me is enough to compensate for my year of work."

But what happens as reproduction technologies improve: as printing presses get quicker, or as the Internet lets teenagers share music files faster and farther? Won't that drive authors and musicians into utter poverty?

In fact, Boldrin and Levine argue, the opposite should occur. Increasing rates of reproduction will drop marginal production costs and, therefore, prices. If demand for the good is elastic—that is, if demand rises disproportionately when prices drop—then total revenue will increase. And since creators with strong rights of first sale are paid the current value of future revenue, their pay will climb. "The point we're making is the invention of things like Napster or electronic publishing and so on are actually creating more opportunities for writers, musicians, for people in general to produce intellectual value, to sell their stuff and actually make money," says Boldrin. "The costs I suffer to write down one of my books or songs have not changed, so overall we actually have a bigger incentive, not smaller incentive."

Conventional wisdom admits that monopoly rights impose short-term costs on an economy. They give an undue share of the economic pie to those who own copyrights and patents; they misallocate resources by allowing innovators to command too high a price; they allow innovators to produce less than the socially optimal level of the new invention. But these costs are all considered reasonable because innovation creates economic growth: The static costs are eclipsed by dynamic development.

Boldrin and Levine say this is a false dilemma. Monopoly rights are not only unnecessary for innovation but may stifle it, particularly when an innovation reduces the cost of expanding production. "Monopolists as a rule do not like to produce much output," they write. "Insofar as the benefit of an innovation is that it reduces the cost of producing additional units of output but not the cost of producing at the current level, it is not of great use to a monopolist." Monopolists, after all, can set prices and quantities to maximize their profits; they may have no incentive to find faster reproduction technologies. More broadly, producers are likely to engage in what economists call "rent-seeking behavior"—efforts to protect or expand turf (and profits) by fighting for government-granted monopoly protection—and that behavior is likely to stifle innovation. Expensive patent races, defensive patenting (in which firms create a wall of patents to prevent competitors from coming up with anything remotely resembling their product), and costly infringement battles are common functions of corporate law departments. Such activity chokes off creative efforts by others, particularly the small and middle-sized firms that are typically more innovative.

Property rights for intellectual goods are sometimes too strong; . . . society might benefit from weaker restrictions.

The Critics

Like any radical innovation, Boldrin and Levine's argument has its critics. "We've been presenting it in quite a few key places, and I have to admit that every time there was a riot," says Boldrin. "There was a riot at Stanford last Thursday. It was a huge riot at Chicago two weeks ago. I know it was a riot at Toulouse when David presented it."

A "riot" among economists might not call for crowd control, but the paper does evoke strong reactions. UCLA's Klein says the paper is "unrealistic modeling with little to do with the real world." In a paper with Kevin Murphy of the University of Chicago and Andres Lerner of Economic Analysis LLC, Klein writes that Boldrin and Levine's model works only under the "arbitrary demand assumption" that demand for copies is elastic, so that as price falls over time output increases more than proportionately and profit rises. In the case of Napster and the music industry, this "clearly conflicts with record company pricing. That is, if Boldrin and Levine were correct, why are record companies not pricing CDs as low as possible?"

Romer has a broader set of objections. As a co-author and graduate school classmate of Levine's and a former teacher of Boldrin's at the University of Rochester, Romer has no desire to brawl with his respected colleagues. Moreover, he agrees that property rights for intellectual goods are sometimes too strong; in some cases, society might benefit from weaker restrictions. Music file sharing, for example, might increase social welfare even if it hurts the current music industry. And he stresses that alternative mechanisms for bringing forth innovation—government support for technology education, for example—might well be superior to copyrights and patents. Nonetheless, Romer does have serious problems with the new theory.

First of all, the first-sale rights Boldrin and Levine would assign to innovators "would truly be an empty promise." In their model, if a pharmaceutical firm discovers a new compound, it can sell the first pills but not restrict their downstream use. A generic drug manufacturer could then buy one pill, analyze it, and start stamping out copies.

"So what Boldrin and Levine call 'no downstream licensing' is instant generic status for drugs," Romer complains. And while they argue that the inventor "can sell a few pills for millions of dollars," this is unrealistic if everyone who buys a pill can copy it. "You can make a set of mathematical assumptions so that this is all logically consistent," says Romer, "but those assumptions are wildly at odds with the underlying facts in the pharmaceutical industry."

Patents and copyrights are NOT private contracts; they are monopoly rights given by governments.

If Boldrin and Levine are unrealistic about appropriability, they are even more at sea regarding rivalry, Romer adds. While it's true that ideas must be embodied to be economically useful, it's false to say that there is no distinction between the idea and its physical instantiation. A formula must be written down, but the formula is far more valuable than the piece of paper on which it's written. In a large market, the formula could be so valuable that "the cost of the extra paper is trivial—so small that it is a reasonable approximation to neglect it entirely." If Romer's approximation is right—if it truly is reasonable to neglect that "trivial" cost—then out goes the slim element of rivalry on which the Boldrin/Levine argument rests.

Romer also objects to the contention that competition can deal well with sunk costs. And he suggests that Boldrin and Levine are wrong to object to copyright restriction of downstream use, since perfect competition allows sellers and buyers to enter contracts that impose such restrictions. "What justification is there," says Romer, "for preventing consenting adults from writing contracts that limit subsequent or downstream uses of a good?"

Boldrin's quick e-mail response: "We never say anything like that!! Patents and copyrights are NOT private contracts; they are monopoly rights given by governments."

Romer counters: "The legal system creates an opportunity for an owner to write contracts that limit how a valuable good can be used. . . . The proposal from Boldrin and Levine would deprive a pharmaceutical company or the owner of a song of the chance to write this kind of contract with a buyer."

According to University of Chicago's Lucas, "There is no question that Boldrin and Levine have their theory worked out correctly. The issue is where it applies and where it doesn't." Their strongest examples, Lucas argues, are Napster and the music industry. "If we do not enforce copyrights to music, will people stop writing and recording songs?" he asks rhetorically. "Not likely, I agree. If so, then protection against musical 'piracy' just comes down to protecting monopoly positions: something economists usually oppose, and with reason."

But Lucas cautions that their theory may not apply everywhere. "What about pharmaceuticals?" he asks, echoing Romer. "Here millions are spent on developing new drugs. Why do this if the good ideas can be quickly copied?"

Refining the Theory

Solow suggests that Boldrin and Levine should enrich their "very nice paper" by testing its robustness. What happens, for example, if the time interval between invention and copying is shrunk? And—echoing Arrow—"does anything special happen if you introduce some uncertainty about the outcome of an investment in innovation?"

Boldrin and Levine recognize that work remains to be done to strengthen their theory. They have begun to examine the effect of uncertainty on their model, as Solow suggests, and they say the results still broadly obtain. The difference is that a large monopolist may be able to insure himself against risk, whereas competitors will need to create securities that allow them to sell away some of the risk and buy some insurance.

As for pharmaceutical research and development, Boldrin and Levine contend that their critics are misrepresenting the industry's economics. Much of the high cost of pharmaceutical R&D, Boldrin argues, is due to the inflated values placed on drug researchers' time because they are employed by monopolists. Researchers are paid far less in the more competitive European drug industry.

In addition, Levine says, pharmaceuticals aren't sold into a competitive market: "They are generally purchased by large organizations such as governments and HMOs." If inflated drug prices are viewed more realistically, these economists argue, the development costs of new drugs would not be nearly as insurmountable as commonly believed.

Moreover, copying a drug takes time and money, providing the innovative drug company with a substantial first-mover advantage. "It's not obvious that the other guys can imitate me overnight," says Boldrin. "The fact that you are the first and know how to do it better than the other people—it may be a huge protection."

Still, they admit, there are cases of indivisibility where the initial investment may simply be too large for a perfectly competitive market. "We have argued that the competitive mechanism is a viable one, capable of producing sustained innovation," they write. "This is not to argue that competition is the best mechanism in all circumstances." Indivisibility constraints may keep some socially desirable innovations from being produced; the situation is similar to a public goods problem. The authors suggest that contingent contracts and lotteries could be used in such cases, but "a theory of general equilibrium with production indivisibility remains to be fully worked out."

Some economists have already begun work on the next stages. Quah at the London School of Economics has pushed Boldrin and Levine's model in a number of directions to test its robustness and applicability. In one paper, he finds it works well if he tweaks assumptions about the consumption and production of the intellectual assets, but it falters if he changes time constraints.

In another paper, Quah contends that Boldrin and Levine's potential solutions to indivisibility constraints may not actually resolve the problem. "What is needed," he writes, "is the capability to continuously adjust the level of an intellectual asset's instantiation quantity." Roughly translated: We need the ability to come up with half an idea. That might be a problem.

More studies like Quah's will be needed to poke, prod, refine, refute, and extend Boldrin and Levine's theory. And empirical work will be needed to see whether it is indeed a more apt description of innovation. The theory is part of an intellectual thicket, and economists who work that thicket tend to render it impenetrable by adopting different terms or defining identical terms differently.

What is clear, though, is that Boldrin and Levine have mounted a formidable assault on the conventional wisdom about innovation and the need to protect intellectual property. That it has met with opposition or incredulity is to be expected. What matters are the next steps.

"The reaction for now is surprise and disbelief," Boldrin says. "We'll see. In these kinds of things, the relevance is always if people find the suggestion interesting enough that it's worth pushing farther the research. All we have made is a simple theoretical point."

Avoiding Intellectual Property Disputes[2]

BY LIEN VERBAUWHEDE
INTERNATIONAL TRADE FORUM, NOVEMBER/DECEMBER 2002

Intellectual Property Created by Employees

Businesses often rely on employees or independent consultants to develop their intellectual property assets and assume that they automatically own the intellectual property rights on the resulting creations. However, this is not always the case.

Many employees create intellectual property in the course of their employment. This may be a software programme, article, architect's plans, new logo, new product or product packaging, business plan, invention or many other types of creative work. But who owns the rights to these materials: the creator or the employer? The answer varies from one country to another and even within a given country, it may depend on the law and the employer/employee relationship.

Inventions

In many countries, the employer owns an invention made by an employee if it is related to the employer's business, unless the employment contract stipulates otherwise. Conversely, in some countries the rights to inventions belong to the inventor, unless otherwise agreed. In other countries, for example the United States, the employee may retain the right to exploit the invention, but the employer has non-exclusive rights to use the invention for internal purposes. This is known as "shop rights."

Some countries grant employees the right to a reasonable compensation for inventions, whereas other countries do not grant any remuneration whatsoever, or only limited remuneration in exceptional cases.

Copyright

In most countries, if an employee produces a literary or artistic work, the employer automatically owns the copyright, unless otherwise agreed. But in some countries, the transfer of rights is not automatic. There are several circumstances under which an

2. Article by Lien Verbauwhede from *International Trade Forum* November/December 2002. Reproduced from the magazines of the International Trade Centre (an agency of the United Nations and the World Trade Organization) and the World Intellectual Property Organization (*http://www.wipo.int/sme/en/index.html*).

employee may own all or part of the rights. For example, if the employer is a publisher, the employee will, in most countries, own the copyright for some purposes, such as the publication of a book, and the employer owns the copyright for other purposes. In other countries, if an employee generates software in the course of employment, he or she owns the copyright, unless otherwise stated in the employment contract.

The moral rights—i.e., the rights to claim authorship and to oppose changes to the work that could harm the creator's reputation—are not transferable. They remain with the author, even if he or she has transferred ownership of the economic rights to the employer. In some countries, such as the U.S. and Canada, moral rights can be waived.

Industrial Designs

Generally, design rights belong to the employer. In some countries, however, employees retain the right of ownership, unless otherwise agreed. In some cases, the employer has to pay the employee an equitable reward, which takes into account the economic value of the industrial design and any benefit the employer derives from using it. In other countries, the creator of an industrial design remains the proprietor unless he or she has received a reward for it.

Intellectual Property Created by Independent Contractors

Companies regularly engage consultants or independent contractors to create material for them. In this case, both the company and the independent contractor should take care to address the question of ownership of intellectual property assets. For example, they need to decide, if the contractor presents a number of designs or logos and the company accepts only one, who owns the intellectual property rights over the remaining options.

Inventions

In most countries, an independent contractor hired to develop a new product or process owns all rights to the invention, unless agreed otherwise. This means that, unless the contractor has a written agreement with the company giving ownership of the invention to that company, the company will have no ownership rights, even if it paid for the development process.

Copyright

In most countries, a freelance creator owns the copyright, unless he has signed a written agreement that this is "work for hire." If there is such a written agreement, the company owns the intellectual property, but the moral rights remain with the author. In the

Practical Guidelines for Small and Medium Enterprises (SMEs)

Below are a few "golden rules" to avoid disputes with employees or independent contractors:

1. **Obtain legal advice**. As with most legal matters, it is essential to get skilled advice before entering into any agreement with employees or independent contractors.
2. **Conclude a written agreement**. Agree on who owns the intellectual property rights to any material created by an employee or independent contractor, whether and when transfer of ownership will take place, who has the right to exploit it, who is to pay for it, whether improvements or modifications are allowed, etc. Make sure that the agreement is valid under the applicable intellectual property laws.
3. **Draw up a contract before work is started**. Make sure that you deal with intellectual property ownership issues before collaboration starts, as even the earliest stages of work can give rise to intellectual property issues.
4. **Include confidentiality clauses in all contracts**. Include "non-competition" clauses in contracts, as today's employees may be tomorrow's competitors.
5. **Adopt internal policies and regulations or guidelines on employee inventions.** Such policies and regulations should contain provisions on matters including: the categories of inventions that fall within the field of the employer's business; the employee inventor's obligation to notify the employer of inventions; the employer's procedures for handling such notifications; confidentiality requirements and patent prosecution; and remuneration for the inventor. Such regulations should be in line with the applicable national intellectual property laws.
6. **Take special care when outsourcing research and development (R&D)**. Ensure that all persons involved sign an agreement whereby they give the company sufficient rights to the results of their work. Companies should ensure that all rights to the results of the project are transferred to them, including the right to re-transfer the rights and to make alterations, if the project produces materials eligible for copyright protection. R&D agreements should also contain provisions conferring the rights to know-how, copyright for research reports, and rights over physical material and background information, which is not within the public domain.

All this should be kept strictly confidential.

absence of such an agreement, the person who paid for the work is generally entitled to use the work only for the purpose for which it was created. Companies that have paid an independent contractor to create a web site for them may be unpleasantly surprised to find they do not own the creation. Different rules may apply for commissioned photographs, films and sound recordings.

Industrial Designs

If a freelance designer produces a design, the intellectual property rights will not pass automatically to the commissioning party, but will remain with the freelance designer. In some countries, the commissioning party owns the rights to a design only if a reward has been paid for it.

Fair Use and Abuse[3]

BY GARY STIX
SCIENTIFIC AMERICAN, JANUARY 2003

The Big Red Shearling toy bone allows dog owners to record a short message for their pet. Tinkle Toonz Musical Potty introduces a child to the "magical, musical land of potty training." Both are items on Fritz's Hit List, Princeton University computer scientist Edward W. Felten's Web-based collection of electronic oddities that would be affected by legislation proposed by Democratic Senator Ernest "Fritz" Hollings of South Carolina. Under the bill, the most innocent chip-driven toy would be classified as a "digital media device," Felten contends, and thereby require government-sanctioned copy-protection technology.

The Hollings proposal—the Consumer Broadband and Digital Television Promotion Act—was intended to give entertainment companies assurance that movies, music and books would be safe for distribution over broadband Internet connections or via digital television. Fortunately, the outlook for the initiative got noticeably worse with the GOP victory this past November. The Republicans may favor a less interventionist stance than requiring copy protection in talking dog bones. But the forces supporting the Hollings measure—the movie and record industries, in particular—still place unauthorized copying high on their agenda.

The bill was only one of a number that were introduced last year to bolster existing safeguards for digital works against copyright infringement. The spate of proposed legislation builds on a foundation of anti-piracy measures, such as those incorporated into the Digital Millennium Copyright Act, passed in 1998, and the No Electronic Theft Act, enacted in 1997, both of which amend the U.S. Copyright Act.

The entertainment industry should not feel free just yet to harass users and makers of musical potties. Toward the end of the 2002 congressional year, Representative Rick Boucher of Virginia and Representative Zoe Lofgren of California, along with co-sponsors, introduced separate bills designed to delineate fair use for consumers of digital content. Both the Boucher and Lofgren bills look to amend existing law to allow circumvention of protection measures if a specific use does not infringe copyright. Moreover, the Lofgren bill would let consumers perform limited duplications of legally owned works and transfer them to other media.

Fair Use

One of the rights accorded to the owner of copyright is the right to reproduce or to authorize others to reproduce the work in copies or phonorecords. This right is subject to certain limitations found in sections 107 through 118 of the copyright act (title 17, U.S. Code). One of the more important limitations is the doctrine of "fair use." Although fair use was not mentioned in the previous copyright law, the doctrine has developed through a substantial number of court decisions over the years. This doctrine has been codified in section 107 of the copyright law.

Section 107 contains a list of the various purposes for which the reproduction of a particular work may be considered "fair," such as criticism, comment, news reporting, teaching, scholarship, and research. Section 107 also sets out four factors to be considered in determining whether or not a particular use is fair:

1. the purpose and character of the use, including whether such use is of commercial nature or is for nonprofit educational purposes;
2. the nature of the copyrighted work;
3. the amount and substantiality of the portion used in relation to the copyrighted work as a whole; and
4. the effect of the use upon the potential market for or value of the copyrighted work.

The distinction between "fair use" and infringement may be unclear and not easily defined. There is no specific number of words, lines, or notes that may safely be taken without permission. Acknowledging the source of the copyrighted material does not substitute for obtaining permission.

The 1961 *Report of the Register of Copyrights on the General Revision of the U.S. Copyright Law* cites examples of activities that courts have regarded as fair use: "quotation of excerpts in a review or criticism for purposes of illustration or comment; quotation of short passages in a scholarly or technical work, for illustration or clarification of the author's observations; use in a parody of some of the content of the work parodied; summary of an address or article, with brief quotations, in a news report; reproduction by a library of a portion of a work to replace part of a damaged copy; reproduction by a teacher or student of a small part of a work to illustrate a lesson; reproduction of a work in legislative or judicial proceedings or reports; incidental and fortuitous reproduction, in a newsreel or broadcast, of a work located in the scene of an event being reported."

Copyright protects the particular way an author has expressed himself; it does not extend to any ideas, systems, or factual information conveyed in the work.

The safest course is always to get permission from the copyright owner before using copyrighted material. The Copyright Office cannot give this permission.

When it is impracticable to obtain permission, use of copyrighted material should be avoided unless the doctrine of "fair use" would clearly apply to the situation. The Copyright Office can neither determine if a certain use may be considered "fair" nor advise on possible copyright violations. If there is any doubt, it is advisable to consult an attorney.

Source: Library of Congress, Copyright Office, FL-102, June 1999

The divisions that pit the entertainment industry against fair-use advocates should lay the groundwork for a roiling intellectual-property debate this year. Enough momentum exists for some of these opposing bills to be reintroduced in the new Congress. But, for once, consumers, with the support of information technology and consumer electronics companies, will be well represented. In addition to the efforts of Boucher and Lofgren, grassroots support has emerged. Digitalconsumer.org formed last year to combat new protectionist legislative proposals and to advocate alteration of the DMCA to promote digital fair use. The group has called for guarantees for activities such as copying a CD to a portable MP3 player and making backup copies, which are illegal under the DMCA, if copy protection is violated.

The DMCA has not only undercut fair use but also stifled scientific investigations. Felten and his colleagues faced the threat of litigation under the DMCA when they were about to present a paper on breaking a copy-protection scheme, just one of several instances in which the law has dampened computer-security research (see the Electronic Frontier Foundation's white paper, "Unintended Consequences": *www.eff.org/IP/DMCA/20020503_dmca_consequences.html*). The legal system should try to achieve a balance between the rights of owners and users of copyrighted works. An incisive debate is urgently needed to restore that balance.

Open-Source Software Development[4]

BY GEORG VON KROGH
MIT SLOAN MANAGEMENT REVIEW, SPRING 2003

Open-source software development projects—Internet-based communities of software developers who voluntarily collaborate in order to develop software that they or their organizations need—have become an important economic and cultural phenomenon. Sourceforge.net, a major infrastructure provider and repository for such projects, lists more than 10,000 of them and more than 300,000 registered users. The digital software products emanating from such projects are commercially attractive and widely used in business and government (by IBM, NASA and the German government, to name just a few). Because such products are deemed a "public good"—meaning that one person's use of them does not diminish another's benefits from them—the open-source movement's unique development practices are challenging the traditional views of how innovation *should* work.

A Brief History

In the 1960s and 1970s, software development was carried out mostly by scientists and engineers working in academic, government and corporate laboratories. They considered it a normal part of their research culture to freely exchange, modify and build upon one another's software, both individually and collaboratively. In 1969, the U.S. Defense Advanced Research Projects Agency (DARPA) established the ARPAnet, the first transcontinental, high-speed computer network. ARPAnet allowed developers to exchange software code and other information widely, easily, swiftly and cheaply. It grew in popularity and eventually linked several universities, defense contractors and research laboratories. However, its limits soon became apparent. The network could connect approximately 250 hosts, too few to cater to the growing communication needs among engineers and academics. A number of technological advancements that emerged between 1940 and 1970 led to the development of the Internet project that would eventually solve this bottleneck. Today the Internet has more than 100 million users worldwide and has become the major breeding ground for open-source software development.

4. Reprinted from "Open-Source Software Development" by Georg von Krogh, *MIT Sloan Management Review*, Spring 2003, pp. 14–18, by permission of publisher.

The communal culture was strongly present among a group of programmers at the MIT Artificial Intelligence Laboratory in the 1960s and 1970s. In the 1980s, this group received a major jolt when MIT licensed some of the code to a commercial software firm, which promptly restricted access to the source code of that software, and hence prevented noncompany personnel—including MIT hackers who had participated in developing it—from continuing to use it as a platform for further learning and development.

Richard Stallman, an accomplished programmer at the Artificial Intelligence Laboratory, was rather distraught and somewhat offended by this loss of access to communally developed code, and he lamented a general trend in the software world towards the development of proprietary packages that could not be studied or modified by others. In 1985, he founded the Free Software Foundation with the intention to develop and diffuse a legal mechanism that would allow developers to preserve the "free" status of their software by using their own copyright to grant software licenses that would guarantee a number of rights to *all* future users. The basic license developed by Stallman, in order to implement this

The free software idea did not immediately become mainstream; industry was actually rather suspicious of it.

idea, was the General Public License or GPL. The basic rights transferred to those possessing a copy of free software included the right to use it at no cost, the right to study and modify its "source code," and the right to distribute modified or unmodified versions to others at no cost.

The free software idea did not immediately become mainstream; industry was actually rather suspicious of it. For example, firms feared the possible "viral effects" of the GPL license, meaning that, after software in the GPL regime is combined with proprietary software, it would prove difficult to restrict user access through normal licensing or controlling the source code. In 1998, Bruce Perens and Eric Raymond agreed that a significant part of the problem resided in Stallman's term "free" software. The term might understandably have an ominous ring to it when heard by individuals in the business world. Accordingly, they, along with other prominent hackers, founded the "open source" software movement. Open-source software incorporates essentially the same licensing practices as those pioneered by the free software movement, covering free redistribution of software and the inclusion of the source code of a program. These licensing practices also apply to derived works in that the rights attached to the original program apply to all who build upon the source code, without these programmers needing to provide additional licenses.

Incentives to Innovate

Under the aegis of open-source licensing practices, which guarantee that the products cannot be withheld from anyone's use, what are the incentives to innovate, and, given that most open-source projects exist outside the firm's boundaries, how does this innovation process work?

People and firms innovate because there are private incentives to do so. For example, entrepreneurs use their own funds to develop knowledge and products that generate revenue streams (and employees are paid for their creative services to the company). Society also encourages innovation by putting in place mechanisms to protect intellectual property associated with products, so that future revenue streams can be guaranteed for the innovator.

However, a central question raised by the success of open-source software development has been succinctly stated by two economists, Josh Lerner and Jean Tirole: "Why should thousands of top-notch programmers contribute freely to the provision of a public good?" Open-source software developers are rarely paid for their services,

Open-source software developers are rarely paid for their services, and the licenses and hacker practices make it difficult . . . for these developers to appropriate returns from their products.

and the licenses and hacker practices make it difficult, if not impossible, for these developers to appropriate returns from their products. Eric von Hippel and I suggest that open-source software developers freely reveal and share because they garner personal benefits from doing so, such as learning to develop complex software, perfecting expertise with a computer language, enhancing their reputation, and for pure fun and enjoyment. Many of these benefits depend on membership in a well-functioning developer community. Typically, in open-source communities, members give direct, specific and immediate feedback on the software code that others write and submit. This peer-review process is not only valuable for the individual who submits code, but also for ensuring the overall quality of the software.

The importance of community was supported in a study of contributors to the Linux operating-system kernel project. Guido Hertel, Sven Niedner and Stefanie Herrmann found that the more contributors identified themselves as "Linux developers," the higher their level of involvement and the greater their efforts to code for the project. The Linux project and communities surrounding it have the advantage of being well known, and the project's positive image can create a sense of responsibility and loyalty among developers. They also found contributors to be motivated by group-related factors such as their perceived indispensability to the team. Lastly, they found that contributors had important pragmatic motives to improve their own software. This is key to understanding why many skilled software developers work for free. Nic Franke and Eric von Hippel studied the security needs of those who use Apache Web-server security software. They found that because Apache is open-source software, users can modify it to better fit their individual needs and that users who do so are more satisfied.

While these motives explain, to a great degree, the benefits and incentives of becoming involved in open-source projects, the issue of how developer communities protect the fruits of their labor is a subject of some concern. Unlike in commercial development—where intellectual property law protects the rights of authors to appropriate economic returns from their innovations—open-source licenses are designed to guarantee the rights of *future users* against appropriation. Siobhan O'Mahony points out that open-source software contributors have an active concern that their work remains part of the commons, and they zealously protect their work to this end. Open-source project members encourage compliance with the terms of project licenses in various ways. They may exercise sanctioning via online discussions and may use brands and logos to ensure that the intellectual property they have contributed remains in the commons.

The Innovation Process

Open-source projects can be started by anyone with the appropriate programming skills and motives. Typically, an entrepreneur with some workable code or an idea for a software project launches a message on one of the many Web-based collaborative communities, such as freshmeat.net or Geocrawler.com. If others find the code useful or the idea interesting, they join in by contributing code, fixing bugs or other problems in the software, providing comments, ideas, references to other projects and so on. Over time, the number of contributors can grow substantially, and the project may use one of the many technical infrastructures available on the Web to host and monitor changes to the emerging software. The entrepreneurs also normally set up a project mailing list for posting questions and answers or messages pertinent to developing the software.

The first challenge for the open-source entrepreneur is mobilizing top-notch programmers. In some cases, when no viable commercial alternatives exist or when they are too expensive, it may, in fact, be easier to attract top programmers to open-source projects than to commercial development ventures. Developers of standard off-the-shelf software often find it difficult to judge whether a product feature will have a major impact on satisfying user needs, and they also recognize that users often have difficulty expressing their needs. Eric von Hippel has noted that such "sticky" information is costly to retrieve because understanding a user's problems requires that the manufacturer "dwell in the context of the user" for a prolonged period. As a result, the high development (and marketing) costs for standard packaged software typically cause software firms to spread these costs among a large population of users. Companies will therefore seek information about "average user needs and problems," and this affects product development. In some cases, companies supplement this with help from external opinion leaders in order to ultimately strengthen the product design and identify bugs in early releases. For some types of software, this way of optimizing the innovation process leads to market failure and will spur the interest of developers in joining open-source software projects, in which they can code to meet their own practical and technical needs.

Another challenge for open-source entrepreneurs, as has been discussed by Michael Cusumano, is organizing the innovation process properly. For-profit programming companies often seek to reduce development costs and control quality by closely monitoring what programmers do and how they do it. To secure returns on investment in innovation, most companies try to seek out and recruit the most outstanding software talent, bind them by contract and take steps to minimize opportunism. (R.D. Austin has explored in detail the relationship between the software developer and the firm.) Additionally, software companies attempt to contain costs as well as prevent spillover of knowledge, technology and other secrets to competitors by encouraging specialization and division of labor among developers.

The relationship between the open-source software project and its participants is largely voluntary and not regulated by formal contract.

By contrast, the relationship between the open-source software project and its participants is largely voluntary and not regulated by formal contract. The initiator of a project might become well known in the public domain, such as Linus Torvalds who created the Linux operating-system kernel (the central module responsible for such functions as memory, process and disk management); but an initiator cannot legally force participants to continue or increase their efforts in the project. Recent work by Karim Lakhani and Eric von Hippel and by Jae Yun Moon and Lee Sproull shows that contributors to open-source software projects value a sense of ownership and control over the work product—something they do *not* experience in programming work carried out for hire. For this reason (among others), participants of open-source software projects also do not take any particular action to minimize "free riding" (the downloading or "consumption" of remote files without reciprocal uploading or "production" of useful contributions). Project learning in the open-source world is captured in the chronology of e-mail exchanges and in the source code that is open for all to see; there is no need to contain or merge information according to a formal division of labor. By means of this transparency, a project accumulates the development efforts of volunteer users and seems to encourage the software's diffusion in order to build a developer's reputation and spread the products.

Whereas a firm may secure the best talent through the processes of professional recruiting, there is no formal recruiting in open-source software projects. This could lead to less talented individuals participating in open-source endeavors and eventually to compromises in the quality of the software. But research has shown that developer communities are meritocracies, in which technical knowledge and expertise determine a contributor's impact on the software design. Sebastian Spaeth, Karim Lakhani and I studied a sophisticated peer-to-peer software project named Freenet and found that only 30 people had the right to include code in the official version of the software. To become one of these core developers, participants had to demonstrate a considerably higher level of technical activity than other contributors. The open-source organization also self-allocates talent. As noted in our work, as well as in two other studies by Stefan Koch and Georg Schneider and by Bruce Kogut and Anca Metiu, people are not assigned tasks on the basis of predefined labor schemes, instructions and directives, but rather on the basis of interest and self-selection. This drives a high level of specialization, but implies that potentially useful software modules may never be developed.

A View to the Future

What does the open-source software phenomenon imply for future business activities? In the short to medium term, some managers may encourage the use of open-source software in their own firms. Others may attempt to build a business based on distributing and servicing open-source software. U.S.-based Red Hat and German-based SuSE, which distribute Linux software, serve as templates for such activity. Other companies may sell computer hardware running open-source software, such as IBM, which offers Linux as an option. Managers may also try to reduce development costs and boost software standards by using the open-source software development model. Such an example is Sun Microsystems' decision to rely on open-source methods to develop and distribute Java.

The open-source software movement also provides important management lessons regarding the most effective ways to structure and implement innovation. There are potentially great advantages (and perhaps some disadvantages) to a model whereby resources used for innovation are widely distributed throughout the world. The lessons of open-source projects demonstrate the value of specialization through self-selection and how norms of meritocracy and peer recognition help ensure product quality. To be sure, finding the right blend of incentives to encourage innovation is not an easy task. In the long run, however, managers may recognize that offering a mix of motives is the best way to encourage innovation: a mix that ranges from extrinsic and monetary-based incentives to the fulfillment of more intrinsic needs, such as enhanced reputation among peers and community identification—that is, a sense of belonging.

Referenced Research

J. Lerner and J. Tirole, "The Simple Economics of Open Source" NBER working paper no. w7600 (Cambridge, Massachusetts: National Bureau of Economic Research, March 2000)
A foundational paper for research on open-source software, arguing that individuals contribute to open-source software in accordance with career incentives.

E. von Hippel and G. von Krogh, "Exploring the Open Source Software Phenomenon: Issues for Organization Science" *Organization Science* 14, no. 2 (2003, in press)
The authors suggest that a combination of private and community-related benefits results from contributions to open-source software development projects.

G. Hertel, S. Niedner, and S. Herrmann, "Motivation of Software Developers in Open Source Projects: An Internet-Based Survey of Contributors to the Linux Kernel" *Research Policy* 32 (2003, in press)
The authors test two extant models from the social sciences. The first explains incentives to participate in social movements, and the second deals with motivational processes in small work teams, particularly "virtual teams." The authors report a good fit between models and data derived from a survey of 141 contributors to the Linux kernel.

N. Franke and E. von Hippel, "Satisfying Heterogeneous User Needs via Innovation Toolkits: The Case of Apache Security Software" ***Research Policy*** **32 (2003, in press)**
The authors explore a frequently cited reason for contributing to open-source software: People innovate to better satisfy their own needs.

S. O'Mahony, "Guarding the Commons: How Open-Source Contributors Protect Their Work" ***Research Policy*** **32 (2003, in press)**
An ethnographic study in which the author explores the various ways open-source project members encourage compliance with the terms of their project licenses.

E. von Hippel, "Economics of Product Development by Users: The Impact of 'Sticky' Local Information" ***Management Science*** **44 (May 1998): 629–644**
Information about user needs and problems is "sticky," in the sense that it is costly to retrieve for a manufacturer. See also "'Sticky Information' and the Locus of Problem Solving: Implications for Innovation," E. von Hippel, *Management Science* 40, no. 5 (1994): 429–439.

M.A. Cusumano, "Shifting Economies: From Craft Production to Flexible Systems and Software Factories" ***Research Policy*** **21, no. 5 (1992): 453–480**
The author discusses the organization of large-scale, commercial software innovation.

R.D. Austin, "The Effects of Time Pressure on Quality in Software Development: An Agency Model" ***Information Systems Research*** **12, no. 2 (2001): 195–207**
The author explores in detail the relationship between the software developer and the firm.

K. Lakhani and E. von Hippel, "How Open Source Software Works: 'Free,' User-to-User Assistance" ***Research Policy*** **32 (2003, in press)**
How users demonstrate satisfaction and obligation in assisting each other in resolving tasks related to use of Apache software. Also see J.Y. Moon and L. Sproull, "Essence of Distributed Work: The Case of the Linux Kernel," *First Mon-*

day 5, no. 11 (Nov. 2000).

G. von Krogh, S. Spaeth and K. Lakhani, "Community, Joining, and Specialization in Open-Source Software Innovation: A Case Study" *Research Policy* 32 (2003, in press)
A study of growth and specialization in a community of developers.

S. Koch and G. Schneider, "Effort, Co-operation, and Co-ordination in an Open Source Software Project: GNOME" *Information Systems Journal* 12, no. 1 (2002): 27–42
Research on open-source projects from a software engineering perspective. The data are used for a first attempt to estimate the total effort to be expended on a particular project.

B. Kogut and A. Metiu, "Open-Source Software Development and Distributed Innovation" *Oxford Review of Economic Policy* 17, no. 2 (2001): 248–264
The authors of this paper argue that open-source software development is a production model that exploits the distributed intelligence of participants in Internet communities.

Suggested Reading

Hackers: Heroes of the Computer Revolution, Steven Levy (New York: Anchor/Doubleday, 1984)

The Cathedral and the Bazaar: Musings on Linux and Open Source by an Accidental Revolutionary, Eric Raymond (Sebastopol, California: O'Reilly, 1999)

Rebel Code: Linux and the Open Source Revolution, G. Moody (Cambridge, Massachusetts: Perseus Publishing, 2001)

Networks of Innovation, I. Tuomi (Oxford University Press, 2002)

"The Open Source Definition," B. Perens (1998), *http://perens.com/Articles/OSD.html*

"Why Open Source Software Can Succeed," A. Bonacorsi and C. Rossi *Research Policy* 32 (2003, in press)

"How Open Is Open Enough? Melding Proprietary and Open Source Platform Strategies," J. West *Research Policy* 32 (2003, in press)

"Institutional Entrepreneurship in the Sponsorship of Common Technological Standards: The Case of SUN Microsystems and Java," R. Garud, S. Jain and A. Kumaraswamy *Academy of Management Journal* 45, no. 1 (2002): 196–214

Attack of the Freebie Software[5]

BY PAUL ANDREWS
U.S. NEWS & WORLD REPORT, OCTOBER 14, 2002

By rights, GiftCertificates.com should be a Microsoft loyalist. Its CEO, Michael Ahern, is a former Microsoft executive. Its business, selling digital gift certificates, was built on Windows database and server technology. Still, the Seattle-based firm is considering switching to free Linux and open-source software. New license fees from Microsoft have put the bite on GiftCertificates' budget. Ahern won't supply an exact figure but says the difference "is hundreds of dollars on the Linux side versus tens of thousands of dollars for Windows."

Ahern is hardly alone in his dilemma. Chafing under what they call the "Microsoft tax"—license fees collected each time they upgrade personal computers and server networks—customers from the government of China to Europe's Ford Motor Co. division are switching to free software systems. Linux's penguin logo is cropping up all over. "Developing countries, software developers, [and] schools are embracing Linux more," says Phil Mogavero, president of Data Systems Worldwide, technology consultants. "Linux has the capability of creating a paradigm shift."

Posturing

So far, Microsoft is unruffled. "We don't see a Linux revolution happening out there," says Peter Houston, the software giant's chief server strategist. In his view, a lot of Linux advocacy is posturing by Microsoft customers hoping to negotiate a break on license fees. "As much noise as Linux has generated, we haven't seen it translating to people actually deploying it," Houston says. Moreover, Linux isn't as "free" as it sounds, Houston argues. Installation and training costs, ongoing support, and administration fees add up: "They might save on the operating system but get less for their dollar in the long run. It's a bit of a shell game." He cites Target as an example of a chain that converted point-of-sale software to Linux but returned to Windows.

Still, the roll call of customers moving toward open source is growing. IBM is pushing Linux for point-of-sale systems already adopted by Regal Cinemas theaters and Sherwin-Williams paint stores. Federal agencies such as the Federal Aviation Administration and the National Weather Service already use Linux servers, while the National Security Agency is backing a secure version. Governments

5. Copyright © 2002 *U.S. News & World Report*, L.P. Reprinted with permission.

from Germany and France to Mexico and Peru are studying open-source alternatives. China is working on an official "Red Flag" Linux version, and Taiwan is also promoting a localized variant. Microsoft plans a $750 million campaign in China, and Chairman Bill Gates recently flew to Peru to make a $550,000 donation—widely seen as efforts to blunt Linux's popularity by wooing young developers overseas. "The market has fundamentally changed from 'Is Linux for real?' to an understanding of open source's value to an overall software strategy," says IBM's John Sarsgard, head of worldwide Linux sales.

The roll call of customers moving toward open source is growing.

Based on its kinship to Unix, the freely distributed operating system from AT&T that provided the Internet's underpinnings, Linux has long been popular with developers and on college campuses. Last year Apple released its new Macintosh OS X operating system built on another Unix variant. "All the alpha geeks I know are running OS X," says Tim O'Reilly, a Unix book publisher. One reason is convenience: Developers who once did "real work" on Unix but needed a Windows computer for office tasks now can combine both pursuits in a single machine and operating system, O'Reilly notes. Ironically, Microsoft largely made the switch possible since its Office X software runs on Mac OS X. "If Microsoft pulls the plug on Office X, we'll know Linux is having a real impact," O'Reilly says.

As a network and Internet technology, Linux runs on more than 1 of every 4 servers, trailing only Microsoft's nearly 49 percent share of the server market. By contrast, Linux adoption on the desktop is still rare. It seldom comes preinstalled like Windows and uses unfamiliar text commands to get up and running. Windows-like interfaces such as Lindows and Lycoris Desktop/LX are available, joining applications suites such as OpenOffice and StarOffice. But reviews for all Linux desktop software have been mixed.

Even so, Linux may be picking up interest from end users. Erica Simon, a San Francisco State University psychology major "fed up with Windows crashing and doing weird things," switched to Red Hat Linux on a Dell notebook computer. She needed help from her programmer fiance but says the learning curve "was not really that hard, and the benefits far outweigh any pain." Hoping to capture Windows refugees, Sun recently announced it would sell cheap Linux PCs. Wal-Mart sells $199 PCs loaded with Lindows, and PC "clone" dealers sell Windows-less PCs aimed at Linux users.

Special Access

To combat the Linux cost advantage, Microsoft is offering to allow governments and universities to access parts of Windows source code and may give top developers access as well. The firm has also extended deadlines for the new pricing structure. And Microsoft still touts itself as the low-cost alternative to packages from Oracle and Sun. "Microsoft still looks good next to Oracle, but I don't think the new pricing structure's impact [on Web businesses] was fully thought through," GiftCertificates' Ahern says.

In a notable tone shift, Microsoft CEO Steve Ballmer last month called Linux "a serious competitor" that is forcing the firm to "justify our posture and pricing." Translation: Microsoft will try to prove its support, service, and reliability are worth the extra bucks. It's an ironic sentiment from a company that built market share largely by bundling or giving away software with the operating system: Today it's Microsoft's turn to complain about having to compete with "free."

Protections on Intellectual Properties Do Differ[6]

BY MAXINE LANS RETSKY
MARKETING NEWS, JUNE 9, 2003

At least once a week, I get a call from someone telling me that they want to patent something. After a short discussion, many times what they really seek is trademark or copyright protection. That tells me that many business people have a hard time understanding the difference between these three types of intellectual property—which is understandable, because it can be confusing at times.

Patents protect inventions and the laws are designed to encourage technology advances and new ideas. The law gives the inventor a monopoly on his invention for a limited period of time in exchange for sharing the technology when the patent expires. One type of patent, a utility patent, protects the functional aspect of an invention provided it is unique. Design patents protect the ornamental aspect of something. Inventors are entitled to protection regardless of whether they use the invention or just prevent others from using it during the life of the patent.

Trademarks are adjectives that identify the source of goods or services with rights in the mark being derived from actual use. Most of the time, trademarks are words, but they can also be sounds, colors or shapes.

Copyright laws deal with the written expression of ideas once they are reduced to a tangible form. You can obtain a copyright for a book, but not for its title, if it is original. Marketers must understand that copyright laws do *not* protect the ideas themselves, only the *expression* of the idea. For example, it would protect an actual manuscript about a dog who could talk, but not the idea of a talking dog.

There are certain things that patents, trademarks and copyrights have in common: All three are personal property, as opposed to real property. In some cases, it is possible to get trademark, copyright and patent protection for the same product. All three types of protection are available in the United States and can also be obtained in other countries, provided all the requirements are met.

For example, a telephone probably has at least one trademark associated with it (for example, the brand name of the phone and possibly the model of the phone). If the phone is unique and the

6. Article by Maxine Lans Retsky from *Marketing News* June 9, 2003, page 12. Copyright © *Marketing News*. Reprinted with permission.

design is not functional, then it may be copyrightable (for example, a phone that looks like a football or a cartoon character). In addition, there may be aspects of the phone that involve new technology and have patents associated with them.

The most important distinction between patents, trademarks and copyrights is the scope of the protection that is offered. Patent protection can only be granted by the government. An inventor cannot claim "common law" patent rights. And the protection that comes along with the patent is determined by the "claims" of the patent. Patent laws do not require the patent holder to use or sell goods under the patent once it issues. In fact, patent holders commonly license others to use the patent, which can be lucrative. The patent owner has a right to prevent others from using the patent, regardless of what he does with the patent.

The most important distinction between patents, trademarks and copyrights is the scope of the protection that is offered.

Trademark owners are only allowed to prevent others from using their marks if there is a likelihood that the use will cause a confusion with the owner of the mark. And, in order to be entitled to protection, the trademark owner must be using the mark. Unlike a patent owner, a trademark owner is entitled to protection whether or not the mark is registered.

Copyright protection is available as soon as a work is fixed in a tangible form, regardless of whether the work is registered with the copyright office or not. However, there are some advantages to having a copyright registration, if you need to enforce your rights against another party.

Copyright, trademark and patent protection all last different amounts of time and have different costs associated with them. Patents expire and are not renewable. Patents also cost a lot more to obtain than trademark and copyright registrations. Even a relatively straightforward patent will run $5,000 to $10,000, while trademark and copyrights can usually be registered for less than $1,000. Trademark protection lasts forever, so long as the mark is in use, and registrations of trademarks can be maintained forever. Copyright registrations last for the life of the author plus 50 years.

How do you decide what type of protection is available to you and what you should have? You should probably not do it without consulting an intellectual property lawyer. Many lawyers will review your potential portfolio without charging you, and it will be time well spent. Once you know what protection is available to you, you will be able to weigh the costs of obtaining it against the advantages of having it. But don't wait too long to do this because you can lose certain rights if you don't seek protection in a timely fashion.

Drug Companies Battle in the War over Generics[7]

BY GLENN SINGER
SOUTH FLORIDA SUN-SENTINEL, NOVEMBER 18, 2001

Florence Rubin of Boca Raton spends $117 a month for a brand-name medication to control a chronic digestive problem. She'd like to find a less-expensive generic drug.

"It's so costly. I don't have a drug plan, and I pay full price," Rubin said.

Her doctor says she could switch to a generic version of Prilosec and save a lot of money. But there's a hitch.

Even though the primary patent for Prilosec expired last month, the company that has developed a generic copy has been stalled from marketing it by the brand-name manufacturer through strategies designed to keep its monopoly for as long as possible.

And even though the U.S. Food and Drug Administration gave final approval on Friday to a generic version of Prilosec, the drug won't be sold right away. It's being tied up in a protracted court fight brought by the brand-name manufacturer.

Strategies such as legal battles might become more difficult to implement—and consumers will be able to save money sooner—if Congress acts to close loopholes in federal drug law and stops efforts by brand-name manufacturers to extend monopolies on blockbuster drugs from six months to several years.

Sen. Charles Schumer, D-N.Y., and Sen. John McCain, R-Ariz., are sponsoring legislation that would limit patent extensions to significant changes in how a medication works and the way it is taken.

The bill also would void an automatic delay of as long as 30 months granted by the U.S. Food and Drug Administration to brand-name manufacturers who claim patent infringement by a generic company. McCain and Schumer propose letting generic makers go to court immediately and have a judge rule on the validity of a brand-name firm's patent.

Tilting the law in favor of patients can't come too soon, said Rubin's gastroenterologist, Owen Rheingold of Boca Raton.

"People just don't have a choice in many cases. Brand-name companies are allowed to charge as much as they want and they use every technique they can devise to keep generics off the market," Rheingold said.

---

7. Reprinted with permission from the *South Florida Sun-Sentinel*.

Top Generic Companies

The top 10 makers of generic drugs, by 2000 revenue, in millions:

1.	Teva	$1,709.4
2.	Alpharma	$921.8
3.	Watson	$813
4.	Ivax	$791
5.	Mylan	$790.1
6.	Andrx	$513.7
7.	Barr Labs	$482.3
8.	Biovail	$309
9.	Sicor	$293.9
10.	Impax Labs	$10.2

"Patients get distressed over high drug prices. They get angry with their doctors. Sometimes they don't fill their prescriptions or they don't take medication long enough because of the cost. That can lead to more serious medical problems," he said.

Costly Innovation

Brand-name companies have used various tactics to maintain a monopoly and keep prices high after patent expiration, the generic industry says. Among them: listing new patents for a drug long after initial ones were issued, obtaining approval for labeling changes that extend marketing exclusivity and questioning the quality of a competitor's product through a petition process.

Name-brand companies say the law already is weighted toward generics firms, whose products represent about half of the prescriptions filled in this country, compared with 18 percent in 1984.

The makers of name-brand products will invest $30.5 billion for research and development this year, more than triple the amount they spent in 1990, according to industry trade-group figures.

The trade group notes that "drug innovation is high-cost and high-risk, and only a small percentage of new medicines ever recover average development costs." Without reasonable returns, companies say, they won't be able to afford ongoing research to develop new medicines.

Mark Grayson, spokesman for an industry trade group, said many people mistakenly believe that drug companies earn profits for the full 20 years during which a patent is effective. But what really counts, he said, is effective patent life—the time that remains after FDA approval.

"Because of the lengthy testing and approval process, new drugs lose almost half of their effective patent protection before they ever reach the marketplace," he said.

Billions of consumer dollars are at stake in the battle for generics. Sens. McCain and Schumer say that if generic drugs enter the market as soon as patents expire, consumers could save at least $71 billion on prescriptions over the next 10 years.

But most generics face a long, winding road to market because of court fights, labeling changes that extend patent protection and citizen complaints the FDA must resolve.

Moreover, under a law expected to be renewed by Congress, brand-name companies have the right to obtain a six-month patent extension by testing their drugs on children. Such testing sometimes has led to FDA-approved labeling changes that extend patents by three years.

Recently, the Canadian government indicated it might set a precedent by overriding patents to get a generic version of Cipro onto the market to treat those in danger of anthrax infection. Washington considered a similar idea to void a patent that expires in 2003.

But Canada and the United States reached agreements with the Cipro patent holder, Bayer AG, to produce more of the antibiotic and lower the price.

Most generics face a long, winding road to market because of court fights, labeling changes that extend patent protection and citizen complaints the FDA must resolve.

Tale of the Purple Pill

Generic manufacturers use Prilosec as an example of how the law can become bogged down—to the detriment of consumers.

Once promoted as the "purple pill" and used for gastric disorders, Prilosec is the world's best-selling drug and the fifth-most-prescribed medication in this country with $4.6 billion in U.S. sales last year. The primary patent expired Oct. 5, but Andrx Corp. of Davie can't get a cheaper generic version to consumers.

In 1998, the brand manufacturer, AstraZeneca, sued Andrx and other companies planning to market a generic and charged infringement of patents related to Prilosec. AstraZeneca claimed more-recent patents protected the drug—including one related to an improved process for bulk production and another that applies to the crystalline form of the drug's main ingredient.

While the Food and Drug Administration gave Andrx final approval on Friday without the court case being settled, the company would not take a chance marketing the generic version until legal action is over, said Elliot Hahn, interim chief executive officer of Andrx.

Price Differences

Average price of drugs, by type:

1990
Brand $27.16
Generic $10.29

1995
Brand $40.22
Generic $14.84

2000
Brand $65.29
Generic $19.33

The generic maker could lose and have to yank the drug, resulting in potentially large losses and shareholder upheaval.

Andrx said a trial is scheduled to begin Dec. 5 in New York City.

In another tactic, apparently unsuccessful based on Friday's FDA approval of generic Prilosec, AstraZeneca and another firm told the FDA in July they were concerned with the generic's stability and its ability to dissolve and be absorbed by the body.

The drug agency took almost four months to investigate that concern. So even if the court case had been resolved in the interim, the FDA's investigation would have delayed launch of a generic version.

Overcoming these obstacles is particularly important for Andrx because, under federal law, the first firm to receive FDA approval for many types of generic drugs gets six months' exclusivity. No rival generics of the brand-name drug can be sold during this time, which boosts profits and helps that company's brand become entrenched in pharmacies.

"We are observing a scenario of total abuse of process at a cost to consumers," Hahn said.

AstraZeneca spokeswoman Rachel Bloom said the company won't speculate on the ultimate fate of the Prilosec patents, but said they are part of a normal course of business for the company.

Concern and Anger

The case of Prilosec, known generically as omeprazole, has stirred concern and anger from groups such as the National Consumers League, Gray Panthers and Business for Affordable Medicine.

"This type of activity—the delay tactics—are going to be escalating as more and more patents come close to expiration," said Linda Golodner, president of the National Consumers League.

"When a patent is up, it's time to let other products, specifically generics, come to market," Golodner said. She estimated that the Andrx generic for Prilosec could save consumers $40 per prescription.

William Nixon, president of the Generic Pharmaceutical Association, calls brand-name companies' tactics "mind-boggling shenanigans." Nixon's group represents 152 generic companies around the world.

"The name-brand companies pay their attorneys millions and earn billions by keeping generics off the market for as long as they can," Nixon said.

But the president of Pharmaceutical Research and Manufacturers of America, Alan Holmer, recently told the U.S. Senate Judiciary Committee that the key pro-consumer drug law, known as the Hatch-Waxman Act, was working well. The act created a blueprint to allow less-expensive generic drugs to enter the market.

Mark Grayson, a spokesman for the group, said criticism of brand-name companies is undeserved.

"We haven't violated any laws or filed any frivolous lawsuits. There are severe penalties for that," he said. "The generic makers want to play up how consumers aren't getting less-expensive drugs, but what they really are worried about is their 180-day exclusivity" when they are first on the market with a product.

Bristol-Myers Squibb has been particularly active in trying to prevent generic forms of its products from getting to consumers.

Bristol-Myers fought Ivax Corp. of Miami, which wanted to market a generic form of Taxol, a potent cancer drug. The brand-name company staved off Ivax for almost three years by obtaining a new patent related to the way the drug is taken. Analysts said the tactic made as much as $1 billion extra in U.S. sales for Bristol-Myers.

Over the next few years, brand-name companies stand to lose huge profits because of patent expirations.

Big-Money Stakes

When they first hit the market, generics typically cost about 25 percent less than brand-name equivalents. But after the six-month exclusivity period often granted to the first generic firm to receive approval, the price drops within the next two years to about 40 percent less because of increased competition, according to the Generic Pharmaceutical Association.

Over the next few years, brand-name companies stand to lose huge profits because of patent expirations. Major drugs with annual sales of more than $15 billion are scheduled to lose protection between now and 2005, according to the nonprofit National Institute for Health Care Management Association.

Eli Lilly's Prozac for depression recently came off patent. Other blockbuster drugs such as Zestrel for ulcers will come off patent this year, while Claritin for allergies and GlaxoSmithKline's Augmentin for infections have patents that will expire in 2002.

GlaxoSmithKline's Paxil for depression, which had U.S. sales of $1.6 billion last year, should come off patent in 2006. But there's no guarantee that more patents, labeling changes, lawsuits or citizens' petitions to the FDA won't delay it further.

That's the concern of officials at Canada's Apotex Inc. and the president of its U.S. subsidiary, Tammy McIntire, based in Weston.

"The opposition to our getting a generic form of Paxil on the market has been very calculated and systematic. They've pulled out all the stops," McIntire said. The original patent for the drug expired in 1992.

GlaxoSmithKline has filed four lawsuits since 1998 against Apotex, claiming patent infringement. Meanwhile, the brand-name firm has listed a series of patents, as late as this year, covering the manufacturing process, new forms of the drug and new indications for treatment.

Attempts by Apotex in federal court to invalidate patents have not gotten very far, McIntire said. A Federal Trade Commission investigation into anti-generic activities has dragged on.

"We get bumped in court for criminal trials. Judges retire on us. Generic drug disputes just don't take a high priority," McIntire said. "If we can just get our day in court, or if the FTC can move forward, we might see some light at the end of the tunnel."

II. Plagiarism

Editor's Introduction

From the practice of sensationalizing events to sell newspapers in the 1800s, to the present-day scandal at the *New York Times* over the promising young writer Jayson Blair, plagiarism has plagued the literary world and academia for years. Whether people realize it or not, somewhere along the line most of them have been guilty of plagiarism; many are just never caught. Some plagiarism is blatant: a sentence or paragraph taken word-for-word and used without a citation as if it belonged to the writer. Other examples are more obscure: an idea or sentence could stick in someone's head from something previously read, and soon pop up in their work without the writer even realizing that it is not original. Some of the most educated and well-respected writers have committed plagiarism. Even church officials have been caught stealing sermons from the Web. High schools and colleges have always had to address the problem of plagiarism, and today, teachers, professors, and administrators are becoming more adept at spotting it. Many feel that it is in the early years of schooling that plagiaristic tendencies are born and that they continue into adulthood if they are not caught soon enough.

What does plagiarism have to do with intellectual property? In a word, *everything*. Plagiarism is a serious breach of ethics which IP protection laws are trying to prevent. When a person plagiarizes, he or she steals someone else's intellectual property—the ultimate violation of IP. The Internet plays a large role in the plagiarism problem. On the one hand, it provides easy access to an enormous amount of information; on the other hand, that very glut makes relocating specific text more difficult for those trying to prove the presence of plagiarism in a book or essay. These days, however, plagiarism via the Internet is easier to detect, with Web sites specifically designed for educators to find and fight plagiarism. Chapter 2 addresses the problem of plagiarism and how it is affecting society today. It discusses specific instances in the literary world and the fallout from these ethical scandals, looks at plagiarism in high schools and colleges, explores ways to detect plagiarism, discusses online sites that help to detect plagiarized papers, and explains how to avoid plagiarism altogether.

The first article in this chapter, "Give Credit Where Credit Is Due: Proper Attribution for Communicators," by Dianna Huff, deals with the general problem of plagiarism in society. Huff offers a few examples of prominent plagiarism scandals—including the highly publicized accusations against Pulitzer prize–winning author Doris Kearns Goodwin, whose plagiarism in her book *The Fitzgeralds and the Kennedys* was recently revealed. One ambiguous topic on which Huff touches is the difference between copyrighted materials and those considered in the public domain, which may be used with minimal or no citation. Huff also gives tips for avoiding plagiarism and protecting copyrighted materials.

While plagiarism is a serious problem among some professional writers, many believe that the practice starts in childhood. The next two articles, "Academic Dishonesty: A Plague on Our Profession," by Kenneth C. Petress, and "Plagiarism," by Denise Hamilton, address the issue of plagiarism in learning institutions. They encourage educators to report plagiarism to officials and ask principals, school boards, and parents to take plagiarism seriously. Hamilton's article also provides specific tips for teachers on spotting suspicious papers; searching the Web to determine if a paper was plagiarized from there; and using software and Web sites to help detect plagiarism.

With plagiarism such a prominent issue on campuses across the United States, educators are looking for any means available to detect and deal with it. A handful of Web sites geared specifically towards detecting plagiarism have provided a ray of hope in this area. John Royce's "Trust or Trussed? Has Turnitin.com Got It All Wrapped Up?" explores this new wave in Web-based plagiarism detection by focusing on one of the main players in the field, Turnitin.com. He describes the two types of plagiarism that Turnitin detects; how well Turnitin and other online sites perform; the struggle to identify plagiarized papers; and the need to be diligent in rooting out violations.

While educators are gaining resources to help detect plagiarized papers, editors of publishing companies, magazines, and newspapers must fight plagiarism on their own. Jayson Blair, an up-and-coming reporter at the *New York Times*, shocked the world when he was exposed for repeatedly plagiarizing stories in one of the world's most prestigious newspapers. In "A Journalist's Hard Fall," Seth Mnookin reports on the Jayson Blair scandal at the *Times*. He recounts the tragedy behind Blair's deceit, describing how top managers at the *Times* overlooked his inconsistencies and ignored warnings about his behavior from their own editors while rumors circulated that their leniency was racially motivated. As history proves, Blair is not the first to plagiarize in highly accredited newspapers. An accompanying sidebar, "The News NOT Fit to Print," lists specific plagiarism scandals that have shaken the literary world in the past.

The fifth article in this chapter, "The *Boston Globe* Media Column," discusses the ramifications of the Jayson Blair incident for all journalists. The writer examines the need for editors to be more thorough, as well as the reforms that individual papers (including the *Times*) are now making so that history is not repeated.

The next article in this chapter, "A Plague of Plagiarism," offers practical advice for avoiding plagiarizing someone else's material. The writer, Mark Fitzgerald, hopes to prevent young and aspiring writers from being expelled from their schools or work places, not to mention suffering the shame and embarrassment that other journalists, writers, and even pastors have experienced, as described in the final article, "When Pastors Plagiarize."

Give Credit Where Credit Is Due

Proper Attribution for Communicators[1]

BY DIANNA HUFF
TACTICS, FEBRUARY 2003

Internet sites offering college term papers for sale have become big business, if recent reports cited at *Plagiarism.org* are any indication. A survey conducted by the Center for Academic Integrity revealed that "80 percent of college students admit to cheating at least once" and recent Gallup polls show "respondents consider a crisis in education and a decline in ethics to be the top two problems facing America today." But, as the following examples indicate, plagiarism is no longer limited to the hallowed halls of academia:

- Pulitzer Prize–winning author Doris Kearns Goodwin shocked the literary world when it was discovered she had "plagiarized other writers' books in her 1987 bestseller 'The Fitzgeralds and the Kennedys.'" (*Boston Globe*, March 24, 2002)
- The National Writers Union is investigating whether Yahoo! is selling articles written by freelancers without obtaining permission first.
- When Disney released its feature animation movie, *The Lion King*, the company was accused of plagiarizing "Kimba the White Lion," a popular children's cartoon from the 1970s.

Plagiarism, or using another person's work or ideas without giving credit, is a complicated subject. Because information is free and readily available on the Internet, it can be difficult to discern between copyrighted material and that which belongs in the public domain.

And because the Internet is so large and unregulated, it's easy to misuse copyrighted work. Yet, we are ethically bound to give attribution where it is due—or lose our hard-earned reputations, as Goodwin learned.

Copyright Versus Public Domain

Due to the Internet, we're no longer in control of the distribution of copyrighted content. Professor Pamela Samuelson, in a speech at Duke University's Conference of the Public Domain a few years ago, agrued that content on public Web sites may be protected by copyright law, but it is "available to all comers without fee or apparent restrictions on use."

Indeed, misuse of electronic copyrighted material is rampant—as evidenced by my own experience. A few years ago my client gave me a trade publication article summarizing the industry and technological advances. For some reason, the opening paragraphs seemed oddly familiar, and it wasn't until I clicked on my client's Web site that I realized why. The writer had used content word for word from my client's site—without attribution!

From the Internet and its unfettered access to information has sprung a debate about what constitutes the public domain. (For the purposes of this article, I am referring to what Samuelson calls "information free of intellectual property rights." The public domain, as she mapped out, includes works published before 1923, numbers, symbols, facts, laws, regulations, scientific principles, and other types of information.)

As Samuelson correctly suggests, what constitutes the public domain is always changing and depends greatly on which side of the fence you're on.

"Creativity and innovation always build on the past."—**Lawrence Lessing, author**

For example, Lawrence Lessing, the author of the book *Code, and Other Laws of Cyberspace*, stated in his July 2002 Open Source Convention keynote address, "Creativity and innovation always build on the past." According to Lessing, copyright laws regarding computer software source code inhibit future innovation. He points out that Walt Disney's *Steamboat Willie* is a takeoff of Buster Keaton's *Steamboat Bill* and that the Disney Company is built on feature animation movies based on works in the public domain.

Which begs the question for Lessing, if *Steamboat Bill* had been copyrighted—or Victor Hugo or Hans Christian Andersen—would Disney have an empire today?

So how do you discern between copyrighted material and content belonging to the murky depths of the public domain? Boston-based PR consultant Lyn Chamberlin, president of skyemedia, inc., says, "Everything is in the public domain. And everything requires proper attribution."

Tips for Avoiding Plagiarism

We're all inundated with information from business and trade publications, e-zines, newspapers, TV, and radio—so it is easy to incorporate an idea you've heard or read about without attributing the original source.

This is especially true if you read the same idea over and over. For example, I receive articles and e-zines weekly whose authors tell me, "Don't use the word 'free' in subject headlines or body copy because the email won't get past the spam blockers." I often wonder if I would have to quote anyone if I were to write an article on this topic. Can this fact now be considered common knowledge or part of the public domain?

I would argue that no, it isn't common knowledge; therefore I need to give someone attribution.

To avoid a scandal or any breach of ethics, you must ensure you have given credit where it is due. According to the University of Illinois at Urbana-Champaign's Graduate School of Library and Information Science, you must give attribution for the following:

- Another person's idea, opinion, or theory.
- Any piece of information that isn't common knowledge, including facts, statistics, graphs, and drawings.
- Quotations of another person's spoken or written words.
- A paraphrase of another person's spoken or written words.

University of California at Davis Student Judicial Affairs Web page goes further. Citing Brenda Spratt's *Writing from Sources*, UC Davis defines others' work as "original ideas . . . art, graphics, computer programs, music and other creative expression."

Both Web sites give excellent guidelines for avoiding inadvertently plagiarizing another's work. General guidelines from the UC Davis include:

- Using your own words and ideas.
- Paraphrasing by reading over material first, covering it up, and then writing out your idea without looking at the text.
- Always adding quotation marks when quoting word for word.
- Citing the source and page number (or URL) when taking notes.
- Avoiding cutting and pasting information from the Web directly into documents in progress without noting the source.

Protecting Copyrighted Material

Once you place information on your corporate Web site, it can be difficult to keep track of where it is being used. Other sites will link to yours, content can and will be quoted out of context or misused, and pages can be printed out and photocopied for distribution in classes, lectures, or seminars.

One recommendation is to conduct a search of your company name on the major search engines to see what pops up. If you believe another company or entity is misusing your copyrighted material, contact them and ask them to remove the content or link or to give you attribution. Depending on the severity of the problem, you may have to resort to legal recourse.

Always include a copyright notice on all your materials—including print and electronic media, software, illustrations, and photos. Companies such as Kinko's and one-hour photo shops either cannot reprint certain copyrighted materials or are limited in their service to do so.

Plagiarism is a serious problem. To ensure you aren't inadvertently using others' material, consult scholarly or journalistic guidelines for the correct forms of attribution—and remember to always give credit where credit is due.

Academic Dishonesty

A Plague on Our Profession[2]

BY KENNETH C. PETRESS
EDUCATION, SPRING 2003

Academic misconduct is defined as "intellectual theft" and is seen as endemic in our society. Cheating occurs in many forms and is seen as a precursor to later, more venal offenses. The failure of parents, teachers, administrators, and school boards to maintain a vigilant and proactive stance on academic misdeed is portrayed as a partial reason the practice remains so widespread. A case is made to be more emphatic about rooting out as much cheating as is practical and to make the apprehension process a learning experience so as to teach children why cheating is wrong and not so much to punish them, at least in initial occurrences.

We live in a time when corporate misdeeds are being exposed at alarming rates; when accounting and auditing schemes are coming to light with frightening frequency;[1] and when political claims, promises, and assurances are subject to ridicule and doubt.[2] These lapses in ethics and honesty have not suddenly sprung upon us; they developed over time. Some of the origins of such cultural decay begin in the schools where plagiarism is sadly common and where such dishonesty seems not to be rooted out emphatically and methodically.

Plagiarism is intellectual theft, no less a moral offense than the theft of a car, money, or jewels would be. While intellectual theft is less tangible than other theft forms and other species of academic dishonesty, it is nonetheless very real. Many plagiarizers claim, when caught, that "everyone is doing it," "it's not a big deal," or "I didn't mean to cheat."[3] Such statements suggest that too few people know exactly what plagiarism is; they are unaware of rules against plagiarism; and/or they have learned through benign neglect from teachers, school administrators, school boards, and parents that plagiarism is not a big deal.

Plagiarism and other academic dishonesty take many forms, some familiar to all; others less common.[4] Some of the more familiar such behaviors include: copying test responses from a classmate; taking exams for others; doing another's assignments; not citing others' work included in course papers, take-home exams, or other assignments; and purchasing research papers from compa-

2. Article by Kenneth C. Petress from *Education*, Spring 2003.

nies too willing to sell these to unscrupulous students. Some other less familiar dishonesty methods include: fabrication of quotes and other spoken or written materials with made-up sources; and getting exam copies in advance from accomplice sources. Other academic misconduct sometimes accompanies plagiaristic practices which border on or equate with criminal activity such as: breaking into teacher offices/files to gain surreptitious access to tests or answer keys; sabotaging peers' ongoing work or experiments; and gaining illegal access to school computer data bases in order to alter official grade records.

The author has taken active interest in plagiarism over the years, serving on students conduct code committees over the past twenty years and raising the issue in ethics, persuasion, and interpersonal communication classes as a vehicle of instruction in these courses. Academic dishonesty is familiar to students as validated each year by an almost universal show of hands when students are asked if they personally know others who cheat and/or if they have personally witnessed cheating. When the topic of cheating is raised in

When the topic of cheating is raised in class . . . many students claim not to have been confronted with the issue by parents or previous teachers except when personally caught plagiarizing.

class, few students express heightened interest; many students claim not to have been confronted with the issue by parents or previous teachers except when personally caught plagiarizing. When students have been asked to respond to whether or not they would expose students they knew were cheating, most report they would emphatically not report such behavior. Their typical rationales for refusing to report cheating are: "it's not my job; that's the teacher's job"; "they are not hurting me; only they are potentially hurt by cheating"; "I cannot prove they were cheating, so I'll stay silent"; or "if they need to cheat to pass, who am I to cause them to fail?"[5] This benign neglect of cheating has remained consistent in the author's classes and in individual conversations with students over the past fifteen years.

In many conversations with middle and high school teachers and students, similar responses are given. Teachers at all levels seem to take one of the following stances when probed about their views on plagiarism: "It's too dangerous legally to charge students with cheating"; "It's too much work taking me away from my regular work to bother with investigating, reporting, and defending my accusations"; "Students will just cheat another way if punished and/

or I'll just have them repeat my class next year if I discover and report such behavior"; or "I fear I will not be backed up by administrators, peers, or parents if I do actively act on cheating in my classroom."[6] Cheating is not just a teacher's dilemma; it is a blemish on the institution of learning; it is imperative that fellow teachers, school administrators, school boards, and parents support the detection of and the punishment of plagiarism and other forms of academic dishonesty. Failure to do so vigorously implicitly condones such behavior and severely damages the reputation of an academic institution as well as putting in question the honest efforts of non-cheating students. The case of the Kansas teacher who ferreted out cheating by students under her supervision and who, when severely punishing those known to be guilty by refusing to pass them on to the next grade, was rebuked and reversed by the local school board illustrates the fear and doubt such action engenders.[7] No one else in that school or district is likely to look for or deal with cheating in any tangible way until radical value changes occur.

Cheating is a mindset; it grows like a cancer. When one student "succeeds" at cheating, word of that success is bound to surface among peers. Such behavior is contagious; others will inevitable follow and spread like a disease unless eradicated. The author's experience with students reported to have cheated shows that most of these individuals cheat serially; that is, they cheat in almost every class, every year until caught; and sometimes, even after being caught, they continue the practice until expelled. If a student is apprehended, reported, and severely admonished on his/her initial cheating attempt, there seems to be a chance that this behavior will be curtailed. Word of teacher vigilance of, administrative support for, and board backing of plagiarism detection, reporting, and sanctions spreads like a fire in school gossip chains as do benign neglect or over-lenient teacher, administrative, and board attitudes and behaviors.

Cheating is a mindset; it grows like a cancer.

The value of individual and collective honesty has to be taught, role-modeled, and rewarded in the schools; to neglect or refuse to do so is malfeasance.

Most students want to be honest; dishonesty is not innate; it is learned. Preemptive instruction, role modeling, and rewards must precede the learning of cheating. Such instruction requires teacher vigilance, care not to create circumstances where cheating is easy, available, neglected, or rewarded. Common school teachers must be told by parents in children's presence that they will not tolerate cheating and that they expect teachers to deal with such behavior by any student, including their own, severely if caught. School boards and administrators must be helpful and supportive of teacher efforts to eliminate, discover, and sanction academic dishonesty. Teachers must take cheating seriously and treat the practice consistently, firmly, and humanely, holding values of honesty and integrity as archetypal values.

Lest we believe that plagiarism is exclusively a student matter, consider the following examples: Senator Joseph Biden of Delaware in his 1988 presidential campaign chose to quote British Labor Party leader Neil Kinnock's words without any attribution to the original speaker. His plagiaristic behavior contributed to Biden's withdrawing from the campaign.[8] Such disgrace was not limited to Biden; many people's beliefs that politicians in general are scoundrels were somewhat validated, thus harming the many honest politicians' reputations. Noted historians Alex Haley, Doris Kearns Goodwin and Steven E. Ambrose were accused of scholarly plagiarism in the writing of their books.[9] Such behavior magnifies student cynicism of the view that plagiarism is wrong since famous scholars engage in the same practice. The Reverend Dr. Martin Luther King was accused of plagiarism and there were some who actively excused his behavior as a difference of cultures.[10] Several print and electronic media reporters, too, have had difficulties with plagiarism, including Mark Hornung, editorial page editor for the *Chicago Sun-Times*; Ken Hamblin, *Denver Post* columnist; Bob Hepburn, Washington bureau chief for the *Toronto Star*; Nina Totenberg, National Public Radio reporter formerly of the *National Observer*; and Fox Butterfield, Boston bureau chief for the *New York Times*. Most of these have landed other jobs, adding some truth to the belief that plagiarism is not such a terrible act.[11]

When children experience academic dishonesty in their younger years, they are sowing the seeds for later, more venal cheating of all kinds. Teachers, parents, administrators, and school boards need to take this issue seriously and implement procedures and policies to eliminate as much opportunity for cheating as possible and practical and they need to humanely but forcefully confront misconduct when it is discovered. This must not be done punitively (at least not in initial instances) but be handled so it turns into an educational experience. Highly skilled lessons of this type will likely result in first-time offenses being the last event of its type in such offenders convincing peers not to engage in those practices. The time and effort in rooting out academic misconduct early on will pay rich dividends later on in the lives of our young students as they reach adulthood.

Notes

1. See July 24, 2002, issues of *Time, US News and World Report,* and *Newsweek* magazines for cover stories relevant to business scandals.

2. See any of numerous TV and radio talk shows such as: "The Beltway Boys" on FOX; "The Capital Gang" on CNN; "This Week" on ABC; "Meet the Press" on CNBC; "Face the Nation" on CBS; or Rush Limbaugh on syndicated radio for examples.
3. These quotes have come from students the author has spoken to from his classes and/or in academic dishonesty hearings where the author participated; student names are excised for legal reasons.
4. See Gary G. Neils. (1996). Academic Practices, School Culture and Cheating Behavior. Independent Schools Association of the Central States for an extensive list of academic misconduct behaviors.
5. These comments come from class discussions and written class papers in the author's Communication Ethics class from 1994 to 2001 relevant to reporting plagiarism.
6. These comments come from personal teacher interviews conducted while the author taught university classes in Illinois, Kansas, Louisiana, and Maine. Names of quoted individuals have been omitted for legal reasons.
7. Diane Carroll. (2002, February 8). "Teacher Quits In Dispute With School Board Over Student Plagiarism." *Kansas City Star*, p. 1.
8. Larry J. Sabato. (2002, July 1). "Joseph Biden's Plagiarism; Michael Dukakis's 'Attack Video'—1988." *http://www.washingtonpost.com//wp-specialreports/clinton/frenzy/biden.htm*
9. Paul Gray. (2002, March). "Other People's Words." *Smithsonian Magazine. http://www.smithsonianmag.si.edu/smithsonian/issues02/mar02/presence.html*
10. Theodore Pappas. (1988). *Plagiarism and the Culture War: The Writings of Martin Luther King, Jr. and Other Prominent Americans*. Haliberg Publishers.
11. Trudy Lieberman. (1995, July/August). "Plagiarize, Plagiarize, Plagiarize . . ." *Columbia Journalism Review http://www.cjr.org/year/95/4/plagiarize.asp*

Plagiarism[3]

BY DENISE HAMILTON
SEARCHER, APRIL 2003

When Jennifer was accused of plagiarism by her English professor, her reaction ran the gamut from clueless ("What . . .?") to tearful ("How could you even think . . .?") to righteously indignant ("WHAT . . .??!!"). The instructor, seated at a computer, pulled up a Web page and began reading aloud. There was Jennifer's entire paper, word for word. Determined to cling, however precariously, to the moral high road, Jennifer demanded, "How did my paper get on the Internet?"

Academic dishonesty is nothing new. Sociologist William Bowers, working on his dissertation at Columbia University in the 1960s, surveyed over 5,000 students on 99 campuses, finding that more than half had cheated. Forty years later, new studies suggest the numbers are even higher. Students, when faced with term paper assignments, have variously paid upperclassmen, begged and bribed older siblings, and copied huge chunks of text from journals and monographs that they believed to be sufficiently obscure. Surely these students had teachers in the third or fourth grade who admonished, "When you cheat in school, you're only cheating yourself." But some students just don't care. They claim they are too short on time, or that the assignment is "bogus," or that the course isn't within their major and so it doesn't matter anyway. Some overachievers fear that what they write themselves won't be good enough, and then there is the contingent of students who are just plain lazy. There are also honest students whose plagiarism is unintentional, because they do not fully understand how to summarize, paraphrase, and make correct bibliographic citations.

The Internet has made term paper theft easier than ever before. With billions of Web pages in existence, students can usually find what they seek. And they assume that their professors won't take the time to check, or, if they do, that they won't be able to duplicate the searches and prove that the material was pirated. Wrong on both counts. With cheating more prevalent, educators have learned, unfortunately, to become more cynical. An informal survey at this small liberal arts college revealed perhaps one or two known cases per instructor per semester. For some students, says Donna Decker Reck, assistant professor of English, "Cheating is a way of life."

---

3. Article by Denise Hamilton from *Searcher* April 2003. Copyright © *Information Today*. Reprinted with permission.

Technology has made plagiarism easier, but it has also made it easier to detect. Often an advanced search in Google is all that is needed. Such a search will uncover group project pages, chat and bulletin board messages, Amazon.com reader book reviews, and papers from essay services such as schoolsucks.com. (Who knows exactly how many "cheat" sites exist on the Web? Some of the more infamous include: AntiEssay.com, Cheater.com, BigNerds.com, and ScrewSchool.com. For a list of over 100 free and fee-based paper-writing services, check out *http://coastal.edu/library/mills2.htm*.) It will probably come as no surprise that these sites borrow quite freely from one another. I found the same Shakespeare paper, poorly done at that, on more than a dozen sites.

Technology has made plagiarism easier, but it has also made it easier to detect.

Why have librarians gotten involved? It usually happens like this: An instructor suspects plagiarism and wonders if the librarians—who can find *anything*, after all—can confirm the suspicions. A single short phrase from the paper, unusually pithy for the student writer in question, becomes the search term, and within seconds, the purloined paper is revealed. Word spreads through the departments and before long the library is swamped with requests for help. It makes sense, then, to share our knowledge as information professionals and teach high school and college faculty how to ferret out plagiarized papers for themselves. Some libraries are incorporating plagiarism into the list of topics covered in bibliographic instruction. Libraries are also creating Web pages to provide faculty and/or students with ready reference on the subject.

Hopefully the day will never come when all classroom assignments have to undergo the intense scrutiny reserved for potential plagiarists. In talking with members of the English department at this small college, we pieced together a sort of "cheater profile."

What Makes a Paper Suspicious?

Dogs rarely eat homework anymore but, unfortunately, grandmothers still pass on (sometimes twice in a single academic year!). Modern times call for high-tech excuses: I lost my disk, my printer cartridge ran out, my hard drive crashed. A student who misses a deadline is already under pressure, never mind the added stress of having to produce an original piece of writing. Late papers from students who routinely raise the hard luck story to an art form are suspicious. Likewise, beware the paper borne by a hyperventilating student who bursts into the room 5 minutes before the class is over. Students who habitually wait till the last moment often rely on pilfered prose.

When vocabulary and writing style are inconsistent with other work, a red flag goes up. Sometimes students will insert a sentence or paragraph of their own, which stands out as noticeably different from the rest of the paper. Experienced teachers collect writing samples early in the semester and regularly have students complete in-class assignments.

There tends to be less plagiarism in upper division courses. Students at that level are there, for the most part, because they want to be, and they enjoy the writing process. Introductory courses, required of all students no matter what their major, will more likely include cheaters who just want to get by.

Students who use class time to sleep, read the newspaper, or chat with friends, or who regularly skip class altogether, are more likely to cheat. Students are less likely to cheat when instructors insist on approving topics in advance (and do not allow last-minute changes); review thesis statements, outlines, abstracts, and/or rough drafts; and require photocopies of cited references and even copies of Interlibrary Loan paperwork. Instructors also report less cheating when

---

Students who use class time to sleep, read the newspaper, or chat with friends, or who regularly skip class altogether, are more likely to cheat.

---

they refuse to approve "old" topics (e.g., gun control, abortion) and when they require students to provide personal opinions, not just reporting of factual information. If a student cannot discuss the content of the paper intelligently or does not know the meaning of a word used in the paper, obviously the work is not the student's own.

Cheating and haste often go together. One professor noticed the "cheat" right on the title page. The paper was written for "College Writing II—Dr. Smith" but submitted to Dr. Jones. Look for odd layout and spacing, which occur with the cutting and pasting of Web pages. A hurry-up job may contain evidence of hyperlinks, which will appear grayed-out when printed. Sometimes students print directly from their browsers, forgetting that Web addresses appear on the top or bottom of the page. (As Homer Simpson would say, "Doh!")

Plagiarism isn't always quite that easy to catch. From my observation point at the reference desk, students' top three choices for search engines are Yahoo!, Ask Jeeves, and Google (pretty much in that order). Think like a student and type in a keyword or phrase, and you will very likely get the same list of source documents from which the student could choose. Other sites that are well known to professional searchers but less often used by students include HotBot, Snap, AltaVista, and Infoseek. (Go to *http://www.searchengin-*

ewatch.com for the latest on search engines and how to use them to become a supersearcher.) Meta-search engines such as ProFusion and qbSearch access multiple search engines. (Meta-search engines such as Dogpile, WebCrawler, and Excite are useful, but unlike the previous two meta-search engines mentioned, these three will include advertising in their results—more to sift through.) Students rarely go through the trouble of searching through a long list of documents, so the copied paper will most likely appear toward the top of the results list.

Students do not always copy an entire paper word for word. Michael Bugeja of Ohio University suggests that if a search engine fails, searching not by topic but by phrase can be effective. British spellings—centre, kerb, favourite—are a tip-off, as are British colloquial phrases (for example, "mucking about" instead of the American "messing around").

The word "Boolean," Bugeja points out, means "logical word combinations." So try an illogical combination or an unusual one. A Yahoo! search on Macbeth + witches yields 21,600 results. A Yahoo! search on Macbeth + diablerie yields just 103 hits, many duplicates.

The Software Solution

Several companies produce anti-plagiarism software or offer an anti-plagiarism service. Some can be ordered by individuals as well as by departments or institutions. Visit the product Web site for information about free trials and terms. As of this writing, the major players include the following:

Plagiarism.org
http://www.plagiarism.org

Turnitin.com *(its user portal)*
http://www.turnitin.com

The current market leader in plagiarism detection software, Turnitin.com maintains a database of student papers. The Web site shows examples of how the software works, even when a student substitutes synonyms for almost half the words in the paper or adds sentences and paragraphs. Reports in the form of graphs provide information such as percentage of word substitution. Depending on the size of the college, a subscription can cost anywhere from $1,000 to $10,000, although individual subscriptions are also available.

Glatt Plagiarism Services
http://www.plagiarism.com

This source offers three products that institutions can purchase. The Glatt Plagiarism Teaching Program (GPTeach) is a computer-based tutorial that explains plagiarism and provides practice exercises for students. The Glatt Plagiarism Self-Detection Program (GPSD) is a screening program that students can use to check whether their writing has inadvertently crossed the boundaries into plagiarism. The Glatt Plagiarism Screening Program (GPSP) is available for $250 per copy (licensing is available).

Essay Verification Engine (EVE2)
http://canexus.com/eve/

EVE2 performs an advanced Web search and returns links from which students may have plagiarized, along with a paper copy of submitted material with the plagiarized sections highlighted.

Word CHECK
http://wordchecksystems.com

Word CHECK allows users to build databases of student papers. Pricing varies, depending on the size of database desired.

CopyCatch Gold
http://www.copycatch.freeserve.co.uk

This is a program, not a service, that can work with any language for which it has a list of content words. The program is currently available with English, French, German, Italian, and Spanish lists.

Problem Solved?

Not entirely. Some librarians, as well as attorneys and professors, are raising questions about the legality of maintaining databases of student-written work. For a product like EVE2, this is not an issue because its software searches the Web. Word CHECK and Turnitin.com, on the other hand, retain student papers submitted for plagiarism detection. The more papers collected, the bigger the database.

Word CHECK skirts the copyright, fair use, and privacy issues by placing the responsibility squarely on the shoulders of those who purchase and use the program: "The subjective assignment of '*plagiarism*' or '*copyright infringement*' is within the scope of analysis made by the individual users of the program. . . . All responsibility for obtaining permission to profile a copyrighted document falls upon the user of the program."

Turnitin.com's success—currently its user base numbers more than 400 institutions—depends upon its enormous database of manuscripts (estimated at more than 1 million). The problem is that student papers are copied in their entirety to the database, often without a student's knowledge or consent. This is a potential invasion of privacy. Copying the entire paper may also be a potential infringement of copyright, again without a student's knowledge, since the law automatically gives authors the rights to their work. Retaining student work may likewise violate the Family Educational Rights and Privacy Act. Company founder John Barrie, who created Turnitin.com based on software he developed while a grad student at Berkeley, encourages professors to explain when plagiarism-detection services are used and to request that students upload their own work to the database, so that they cannot later claim Turnitin.com used their papers without their knowledge.

That's not enough for the University of California-Berkeley, which has, ironically, decided not to use the service. Other institutions using the software sometimes have individual faculty members who are troubled by legal and ethical questions and refuse to use it. Still other institutions, however, are enthusiastic about the product. Duke University's own student newspaper, *The Chronicle*, actually endorsed Turnitin.com in an editorial, saying that the "unobtrusive" service "comes the closest to maintaining academic honesty without damaging the trusting environment that administrators have attempted to foster."

Plagiarism will not disappear, nor will the problems associated with detecting it. Librarians can help by sharing their expertise with both students and educators.

Trust or Trussed? Has Turnitin.com Got It All Wrapped Up?[4]

BY JOHN ROYCE
TEACHER LIBRARIAN, APRIL 2003

Almost every week there is a report on the prevalence of plagiarism from Internet sources, or news of a university, school or school district which has tired of student plagiarism and has signed up for the services of Turnitin.com.

Headlines announce: "75 percent of students admit to fraud, studies show" (*Oakland Tribune*, December 9, 2002) or "Using the Internet to catch cheaters" (Newsday.com, December 17, 2002).

Turnitin is reported to investigate more than 10,000 papers a day, and about 3,000 of these turn out to be plagiarized to a significant extent (Paper chase, 2002; Slaton, 2002). Turnitin itself claims that the company gains three new users a minute (Turnitin.com intro, 2002). It is a remarkable success story. As a result, the levels of detected plagiarism are reported to be falling in those institutions which subscribe. It seems enough for a school to announce that it has subscribed to Turnitin for its levels of suspected plagiarism to fall. Turnitin's reputation deters would-be plagiarists.

Two Kinds of Plagiarism

There are two kinds of plagiarism, and Turnitin aims to root out both.

The first kind of plagiarism is from published materials. The original is openly published in some form. The original source might be a book, a newspaper, a television program, CD-ROM, a discussion list posting or a web page. Somewhere, a record exists and it is—at least it was—openly available. The plagiarist found it, and so too might anybody else looking for the same information. In this regard, however, note that Turnitin seeks matches only on the Internet. It does not claim to seek among printed, broadcast or other materials; it searches only the Internet. As more and more students turn to the Internet for their information, this may not, at first glance, be too much of a drawback to the subscribers (Canadian students . . . , 2001; Lenhart, 2002).

Plagiarism of this first kind is traceable. It might take a long time, but because the material was published it should be possible to find the original. However, even Internet sources can be difficult to track down. Search engines search only a fraction of the Internet. Some

4. Article by John Royce, *Teacher Librarian* v. 30, April 2003. Copyright © John Royce. Reprinted with permission.

search only the World Wide Web. Different search engines find different hits, and no single search engine finds everything (Notess, 2002).

A lot of valuable material is found on what has become known as the Invisible Web. Sherman and Price (2001, p. 57) define the Invisible Web as: "Text pages, files, or other often high-quality authoritative information available via the World Wide Web that general-purpose search engines cannot, due to technical limitations, or will not, due to deliberate choice, add to their indices of Web pages." This includes material that is openly available on databases that are free to the end-user. Invisible web pages can often be found easily—but not by the general search engines. Unless one can work out which resources were used or replicate the actual search, refinding the originals may be nigh impossible.

Moreover, many web pages are unstable, here today and gone tomorrow, especially pages published by the mass media. Online journals make their latest pages available, but past issues may be available only to subscribers, or may disappear altogether. Some online journals constantly update their pages. The URL remains but the article vanishes, replaced by another.

A lot of valuable material is found on what has become known as the Invisible Web.

Plagiarism of the second kind is from unpublished materials. These could be personal diaries and letters, a friend's homework, even one's own work originally written for a different teacher last year. Also included is unpublished material passed along a network or fraternity, from one friend to another, from one year to another. This is the form of plagiarism discovered in a well-publicized case at the University of Virginia in 2001, when more than 120 students were suspected of plagiarizing from the same material over five years. Because unpublished work is not openly available, it may be impossible to track down the original material which has been copied and plagiarized.

There is also much concern over the ever-increasing number of cheat sites and paper mills which flourish on the Internet. Some sites do not charge for their services, and may publish the actual papers on the Internet, leading to plagiarism of the first kind, open publication. Papers found on paper mills are expensive and usually at university level. They may even be custom written for the customer. These papers are often sent to the buyer by e-mail or fax, and no search engine will find these materials. They are not there to be found. These lead to plagiarism of the second kind. Curiously, Google Answers may be providing a cheap school-level alternative to the paper mills (Goot, 2002). Even more curiously, Google's search engine (*http://www.google.com*) does not index Google Answers.

All these factors add to the frustrations of the chase.

Enter Turnitin.com

Turnitin aims to track down both kinds of plagiarism.

That said, it is important to realize that Turnitin does not find plagiarism. What it does is find sequences of words in submitted documents which match sequences of words in documents in its database, or sequences of words in documents on the Internet.

Every paper submitted to Turnitin, apart from those submitted as part of a free trial, is added to the Turnitin database. This happens even if no matches to other documents are found. In this way, Turnitin hopes to nail plagiarism of the second kind, plagiarism from unpublished sources. A match will not be found the first time an essay is submitted from a paper mill or an informal network, but if it is ever submitted again, in whole or in part, it will be found. The more schools subscribe to Turnitin, the more papers are submitted and the larger the database becomes.

Turnitin also searches the Internet in an attempt to find source material which has simply been cut and pasted from a published source into a student's essay. Because they are automated, the searches will be more persistent than a human searcher can achieve, and the Turnitin search engine will handle greater numbers of searches than a human searcher.

Many students are incredibly naïve about plagiarism and their chances of getting caught.

Turnitin thus has two strengths: its ability to search the Internet faster and longer than any individual, and the ever-growing database of submitted essays.

And from the press reports published in the open press and the commendations posted on the Turnitin web site, it is doing a good job. Turnitin has seen several rivals come and go. Integriguard and its simplified and free version at HowOriginal.com have disappeared. So too has Findsame, although the original company, Digital Integrity, is still in business. Turnitin has been aggressively marketing itself in the last few years, and its commercial success is evidenced in the headlines cited earlier. The company claims more than 1.5 million new users a year (Turnitin.com intro, 2002). John Barrie, the founder of Turnitin, has declared: "In very short order, we'll have it all wrapped up. We'll become the next generation's spell checker. . . . There will be no room for anybody else, not even a Microsoft, to provide a similar type of service because we will have the database" (Masur, 2001).

Some Nagging Doubts

Some of the reported stories would seem to show that many students are incredibly naïve about plagiarism and their chances of getting caught—and that many instructors are equally naïve. Surprise is often expressed at how easy it is to find essays, to download and to cut and paste. Surprise is often expressed at how easy it is to find the originals when plagiarism is suspected. If only! Many instructors claim they can recognize when a student's voice or writing style changes, especially if a mediocre student suddenly shines. The change may be less obvious when a mediocre student produces mediocre work, and a lot of material on the Internet, and especially on the cheat sites, is mediocre (Royce, 2001).

When plagiarism is suspected, the burden of proof lies with the instructor. The only way definitively to prove plagiarism is to find a word-for-word copy of the original passage or passages plagiarized, and then to show that the student's attribution is missing or wrong. If the match is just a short sentence or two, the student might be given the benefit of the doubt, especially if the rest of the paper is in order. But when large pieces of the paper match other documents word for word with false attribution or none at all, then plagiarism has surely taken place.

The only damning proof is a copy of the original.

It is more difficult to prove plagiarism when there has been much transformation of sentence structure and use of different words. It can be very difficult to prove that ideas have been plagiarized, even when the work is not the student's usual "voice." In these cases, a student who protests innocence might well defend him- or herself successfully. However strong the circumstantial evidence, however unable the student is to explain the research process or to explain words used or provide other "proof" of original work, the case cannot be proven unless the student confesses. The only damning proof is a copy of the original.

And it is quite possible that those whose plagiarism is proven beyond doubt might still fight and beat a reluctant faculty or a weak school board, as happened in Piper School District, following which both the teacher and her principal resigned (Carroll, 2002; Principal . . . , 2002).

Of course, if the instructions are to provide copies of sources used, or to provide full citations and bibliographical referencing, then the student might be downgraded for failing to fulfil all aspects of the assignment. If citations and references are provided then it might be easier to see just how—and if—the original sources have been used. The student's essay might point to a need for more help with the mechanics of research reporting rather than providing proof of plagiarism.

As noted, it is often difficult to find an original source. Sometimes a simple Internet search for the title, a few keywords or a string of consecutive words really does suffice. Many times detection takes longer. The concern is that those who think detection is a simple matter of typing in a few keywords will also think that if no matches are found then the suspicions are not valid.

Similarly, the reports and the sales figures suggest there is great trust in Turnitin. Hildebrand notes (2002, para. 7–8), "The system isn't foolproof, but its very presence in schools seems to serve as a deterrent. 'You don't have to use it,' observes [one teacher . . .]. 'Students just have to know you have it.'" It is another concern that Turnitin's results may be accepted without further questioning; if a match is found then the student is automatically believed to be guilty, while if no match is found, the student is automatically considered innocent. The bulk of comments on Turnitin's testimonials page provide evidence of great and sometimes unquestioning trust in Turnitin's results—and that makes these concerns very real (Turnitin.com Testimonials, 2002).

Turnitin itself does not claim to be infallible. Which is just as well. It isn't.

How Well Does Turnitin Perform?

Several reports draw attention to areas which Turnitin does not cover, and they point to shortcomings in the areas which Turnitin does claim to cover. The fact that Turnitin finds matches in one-third of papers submitted means little, unless one knows that only one-third of all papers written contain plagiarism. A true test of a detection service's detection rate might require a control group, such as a set of papers where plagiarism is known because the investigator has "created" the submission.

This has been done in at least four investigations.

Robin Hill carried out a small test using three completely plagiarized essays. Turnitin failed to find one essay, and found only one of the two sources used to create the second essay. Turnitin failed to find the third essay, but did find a number of false hits, matching strings of words in other papers. Since this last was a paper on recombinant DNA, Hill suggests that the false hits were found because of the limited language available in this field of study (Hill, 2002).

The Joint Information System Committee (JISC) carried out a wide-ranging investigation in several British post-secondary institutions. One of the issues investigated was the success of Turnitin and other detection agents in detecting plagiarism. The investigating team used a number of genuine essays, and also "created" 11 essays from a variety of sources, including paper mills or essay banks. Students were warned before the project stage that their work would be used to test the services. Turnitin performed best of the software and agencies investigated. The JISC report gives Turnitin a five-star rating (excellent) for tracking down cases of collusion, and four stars (good) for discovering cut-and-paste and paper mill origins (Chester, 2000; Large, 2001).

However, respondents to the JISC survey on plagiarism believe that 74 percent of plagiarism originates from textbooks and theses, and only 24 percent from the Internet. At a conference held to discuss the various project reports, there was strong voice for textbooks and also for print and online journals to be included in the Turnitin database (Large, 2001).

The JISC Reports also noted "areas not covered by the project:

- Detection of text converted to a foreign language and then converted back to English
- Detection of essays converted from a foreign language
- Plagiarism of diagrams, pictures or graphs"

and certain other forms of cheating (Large, 2001, p. 2).

My own research forms the third investigation, another attempt to investigate the various plagiarism detection services. My interest grew in part from the realization that many of the papers available on the cheat sites themselves contained huge amounts of plagiarized material, not always detectable using ordinary search engines. I too compiled a number of essays from various sources. It is very easy to plagiarize; could I get away with it? With my plagiarized essays and a number of genuine student essays, I tested various free services, including services which normally charge but which do offer free trial periods. All services showed wanting. My favorite was Findsame, but this company has since collapsed and its services are no longer available.

I found that Turnitin found no matches for material lifted from usenet discussion groups and discussion lists; found no matches for material lifted from online encyclopedias; and did not track down material lifted from journals located in subscription databases. There is irony here, for when much on the Internet is of dubious worth, many librarians encourage students to use the periodicals databases as worthy published sources (Valenza, 2001). Yet these worthy sources are less likely to be detected and a guilty student can escape detection. Nor did Turnitin work well with transformations and paraphrases. In the Piper High School case, one parent reportedly said her daughter "is not sure now how much she needs to rewrite research material before she can use it" (Carroll, 2002, para. 16). Rewriting is not the issue; a piece of work authored by someone else but rewritten in one's own words still needs a citation to the author whose thoughts, if not words, are being used.

On the other hand, it did find matches for small contentless strings of words in completely irrelevant documents. It several times made false accusations of plagiarism, but missed by far the greater part of the material I really had plagiarized, missing 15 of 18 plagiarized passages in one of the essays (Royce, 2001).

Turnitin seeks only one match, and this is a particular concern. As soon as Turnitin finds a match, it stops seeking for other matches for that particular string or section of paper. It cannot distinguish between material used and cited correctly, material for which false citations are made, and material lifted without any citation at all; a match is all, and any match will do.

Also of concern is that a student can quote and cite accurately, but still be accused of plagiarism. If a student does give citations, then the instructor must check them out. This is the first rule of plagiarism detection. The fact that Turnitin finds a passage on a different web site to that cited does not necessarily prove plagiarism. On the Internet, there is frequent double and multiple posting of identical pages on several sites. Of course, if a match is found with no attribution at all, this could be a more definite indication, but it still needs to be checked out.

A student can quote and cite accurately, but still be accused of plagiarism.

The fourth investigation, by Satterwhite and Gerein, is the most thorough survey of those discussed here. This team bought a subscription to a detection service, and their budget allowed them to use papers purchased from Internet paper mills as well as papers downloaded for free. They too compiled their own plagiarized essays, and also submitted genuine student essays.

Their best results were from Turnitin, but they remain cautious about recommending it. They were " . . . not very impressed with the results provided by both the paid and free plagiarism detection services and software" (Satterwhite & Gerein, 2002, Summary of our observations, para. 1). They go on to report: "Based on our findings this far, we are fairly confident in our ability to relate to our faculty that available detection software and services as they currently exist are not effective tools with which to identify online plagiarism. They are not reliable, nor sophisticated enough to warrant the investment of college funds. Not only are they ineffective, but some of the products/services promote a real lack of trust and resentment between professor and student that, especially given their lack of success, makes such a purchase undesirable" (Satterwhite & Gerein, 2002, Preliminary conclusions, para. 1).

Satterwhite and Gerein do report that despite their shortcomings, the detection services performed better than search engines. I would disagree, and suggest that it very much depends on which search engines are used, the skill of the searcher and the source of the material. I always recommend that those seeking to prove plagiarism make sure they include the sources available to students, sources which often include online periodicals databases and

CD-ROMs in any library which the students use; it is also worth looking at print resources in the student's library, journals and books. I believe "an automated search for plagiarism makes the whole thing mechanical. It lacks the nose and instinct, the logic, intuition and determination of a skilled human bloodhound. A skilled librarian may be better able to discover plagiarism. . . . I think it probable that a skilled librarian would have tracked down most plagiarized sequences [from the test submissions], especially those lifted from electronic sources and from the Internet" (Royce, 2001, p. 182).

The comparative studies agree, Turnitin is probably the best plagiarism detection service available but there are still major concerns.

Does It Matter?

Does it matter that Turnitin is less than perfect, when you do not have to prove that the whole of an essay has been plagiarized? Isn't it enough to find that a significant amount has been plagiarized? Indeed it is, and will be, until would-be cheats realize the shortcomings of Turnitin and similar services. They might then use periodicals databases and usenet groups, they might seek out material elsewhere in the Invisible Web, they might well get ever better at rewriting in their own words. They might set out to discover the holes in a detection service's coverage—or read a paper like this. The thinking cheat might well take advantage of Turnitin's offer to check five pieces of work free of charge. If the work passes muster, well and good, and if certain parts of it need more careful handling then this too can be done—and checked before submitting the final product to the teacher.

Innocent students may be falsely accused of plagiarism, and . . . many plagiarists may go undetected.

The bottom line is that innocent students may be falsely accused of plagiarism, and that many plagiarists may go undetected. With these caveats in mind, Turnitin can be used to weed out the most obvious cases, to perform a first sweep. Using it in this way will save much time and worry. But the instructor still needs to check each report, especially when the student has given citations, even if they do not match the sources pinpointed by Turnitin. And then the instructor must still check, or ask the librarian to check, whenever plagiarism is still suspected in other papers which have been given a clean bill of health.

Conclusion

We are not going to beat the cheats. It is too easy to beat the system. In particular, working in a bilingual school and with an international school background, I am all too aware of how many students have two and more languages. If it is difficult to prove plagiarism when a student has heavily rewritten a piece, using own words in place of the original, then it is nigh impossible to catch someone who has translated a source written in one language into a paper written in another.

We can attempt to set plagiarism-proof assignments; we can make it so that students do not want or need to copy; we can devise alternative presentation methods which minimize the opportunity for plagiarism; we can stress process as well as content; we can ask students to provide originals or copies of the sources used; we can make it so hard for the plagiarist to plagiarize that it is easier to do the real work; we can try to promote honorable and ethical attitudes towards work. We can indulge in any number of techniques and strategies which will reduce plagiarism. We can do all this, but we must be aware, we are not going to beat out of existence those who are determined to cheat.

In the meantime, we must also be aware of the shortcomings of plagiarism detection services. They are a tool, a weapon, a deterrent. But they have to be used wisely, with an awareness of their shortcomings. The human element remains vital, and without further investigation of their findings, both positive and negative, innocent students stand to be accused of plagiarism and guilty students could still get away with it. Plagiarism services are a tool, but caveat emptor, buyer beware!

References

Canadian students choose Internet as top homework source, but spend more than half their time searching for relevant information. (2001, October 4). Rogers iMedia Education Group—Press Releases. Retrieved August 6, 2002, from *http://www.rogerseducation.com/press%5freleases/100401.html.*

Carroll, D. (2002, January 29). Teacher quits in dispute with school board over student plagiarism. *Kansas City Star*. Retrieved February 8, 2002, from *http://www.kansascity.com/mld/kansascity/2561083.htm.*

Chester, G. (2000). Pilot of free-text plagiarism detection software: a report prepared for the Joint Information System Committee. Retrieved April 25, 2002, from *http://www.jisc.ac.uk/pub01/pilot.pdf.*

Goot, D. (2002, September 10). Thin line splits cheating, smarts. Retrieved January 2, 2003, from *http://www.wired.com/news/school/0,1383,54963.00html.*

Hildebrand, J. (2002, December 17). Using the Internet To Catch Cheaters. Newsday.com. Retrieved January 2, 2002, from *http://www.newsday.com/mynews/nylied173049335dec17.story.*

Hill, R. (2002). Brown bag lunch: Turnitin plagiarism detection software. Retrieved April 1, 2002, from *http://uwadmnweb.uwyo.edu/ctl/event%5fcalendar/TIINotes.txt.*

Internet plagiarism worries educators. (2001, April 30). Milwaukee Journal Sentinel Online. Retrieved March 11, 2002, from *http://www.jsonline.com/bym/Tech/news/apr01/cheat01043001.asp.*

Large, S. (2001). Notes from the JISC workshop on electronic detection of plagiarism held on the 16 July 2001. Retrieved April 25, 2002, from *www.jisc.ac.uk/events/01/plag%5fdet/sacha.rtf.*

Lenhart, A., Maya, S. & Graziano, M. (2001). The Internet and education: Findings of the Pew Internet and American Life Project. Retrieved June 10, 2002, from *http://www.pewinternet.org/reports/pdfs/PIP%5fSchools%5fReport.pdf.*

Masur, K. (2001, May). Papers, profits, and pedagogy: Plagiarism in the age of the Internet. Perspectives Online. Retrieved June 10, 2002, from *http://www.theaha.org/perspectives/issues/2001/0105/0105new3.cfm.*

Notess, G.R. (2002, March 6). Search engines statistics: Database overlap. Retrieved June 13, 2002, from *http://www.searchengineshowdown.com/stats/overlap.shtml.*

O'Connell, J.C. (2002, May 1). Cliché amendment: Plagiarizers never prosper. The Lantern. Retrieved May 15, 2002, from *http://thelantern.com/main.cfm/include/detail/storyid/248205.html.* Free registration required.

Paper chase. (2002, April 16). The Santa Rosa Press Democrat. Retrieved April 30, 2002, from *http://www.pressdemocrat.com/search.*

Principal in plagiarism dispute announces resignation. (2002, March 17). *Amarillo Globe News.* Retrieved April 30, 2002, from *http://www.amarillonet.com/stories/031702/usn%5fprincipal.shtml.*

Royce, J. (2001, Winter). Quis custodiet . . .: Investigating the investigators. School Librarian 49 (4), 181–183.

Satterwhite, R., & Gerein, M. (2002). Downloading detectives: Searching for on-line plagiarism. Retrieved June 11, 2002, from *http://www.coloradocollege.edu/Library/Course/downloading%5fdetectives%5fpaper.htm.*

Sherman, C., & Price, G. (2001). The invisible web: Uncovering information sources search engines can't see. Medford, NJ: Information Today, Inc.

Slaton, J. (2002, April 29). Plagiarizers beware: Turnitin.com is here to stop your cheating ways. SF Gate. Retrieved May 2, 2002, from *http://sfgate.com/cgi-bin/article.cgi?file=/gate/archive/2002/04/29/plagiar.DTL.*

Tucker, J. (2002, December 9). 75 percent of students admit to fraud, studies show. The Oakland Tribune. Retrieved January 2, 2003, from *http://www.oaklandtribune.com/Stories/0,1413,82%257E1865%257E1041793,00.html.*

Turnitin.com intro (2002). Retrieved June 1, 2002, from *http://www.turnitin.com/*.

Turnitin.com Testimonials (2002). Retrieved January 4, 2003, from *http://www.turnitin.com/static/testimonials.html*.

Valenza, J. (2001, September). What's not on the web. Learning and Leading with Technology, 29 (1), 6–9, 48.

A Journalist's Hard Fall[5]

BY SETH MNOOKIN
NEWSWEEK, MAY 19, 2003

On Sunday, the front page of the *New York Times* featured a uniquely embarrassing article: *TIMES* REPORTER WHO RESIGNED LEAVES A LONG TRAIL OF DECEPTION. The internal report took up four full pages of some of the most valuable real estate in American journalism to recount the sorry history of Jayson Blair, a 27-year-old African-American who resigned from his job as a *Times* reporter on May 1.

A team of five reporters, three editors and two researchers uncovered dozens of errors in stories the *Times* had printed under Blair's byline; the corrections for the stories between October 2002 and April 2003 alone ran almost two full pages, with offenses divided into "whereabouts," "denied reports," "factual errors" and "plagiarism." The second sentence of the story read, "The widespread fabrication and plagiarism represent a profound betrayal of trust and a low point in the 152-year history of the newspaper."

Since he began his career in journalism, Blair has been known for two things: being able to play the internal politics of an institution with uncanny skill and having a problem with accuracy. Those two traits combined in a horrible confluence for the *Times*. Blair's remarkable fraud had come unraveled in late April. The editor of the *San Antonio Express-News* had officially requested that the *Times* investigate a story about the family of a missing soldier that carried Blair's byline, a story that seemed almost identical to one the San Antonio paper had run. After being asked to produce receipts showing he had, in fact, traveled to Texas, Blair resigned; in a letter to the *Times*'s top editors, he apologized for a "lapse in journalistic integrity."

Sunday's story honestly detailed the startling breakdown in communication among *Times* editors about Blair's extensive—and well-chronicled—history of problems with accuracy and sloppiness. The paper was unflinching in its description of how the *Times* failed to track Blair's expense reports and missed glaring warning signs along the way—like the time a national editor saw Blair in the newsroom hours after he had supposedly filed a story from West Virginia. *Times* metro editor Jonathan Landman was quoted as being particularly vocal about Blair; in April 2002 Landman,

---

5. From *Newsweek*, May 19, 2003

the *Times* story reports, sent a two-sentence e-mail message to newsroom administrators: "We have to stop Jayson from writing for the *Times*. Right now."

But there's plenty that the *Times* report, which ran under the rubric CORRECTING THE RECORD, didn't fully explore, namely how a troubled young reporter whose short career was rife with problems was able to advance so quickly. Internally, reporters had wondered for years whether Blair was given so many chances—and whether he was hired in the first place—because he was a promising, if unpolished, black reporter on a staff that continues to be, like most newsrooms in the country, mostly white. The *Times* also didn't address an uncomfortable but unavoidable topic that has been broached with some of the paper's top editors during the past week: by favoring Blair, did the *Times* end up reinforcing some of the worst suspicions about the pitfalls of affirmative action? And will there be fewer opportunities for young minority reporters in the future?

Did the* Times *end up reinforcing some of the worst suspicions about the pitfalls of affirmative action?

"We have, generally, a horribly undiverse staff," says one *Times* staffer. "And so we hold up and promote the few black staffers we have." That's a point other news outlets have made since Blair resigned. Executive editor Howell Raines, who declined repeated requests for an interview with *Newsweek*, told NPR, when pressed about whether Blair was pushed along because of his race, "No, I do not see it as illustrating that point. I see it as illustrating a tragedy for Jayson Blair." (Blair, whose voice mail at the *Times* was still active as of Saturday evening, did not respond to a message left there or on his cell phone; several sources at the *Times* say he is currently in a hospital setting dealing with personal problems.)

Blair's close mentoring relationship with *Times* managing editor Gerald Boyd, who is also black, was not explored in depth in the paper. Blair wrote Boyd's biographical sketch in the *Times's* internal newsletter when Boyd was named managing editor. Blair was known to brag about his close personal relationships with both Boyd and Raines, and the young writer frequently took cigarette breaks with Boyd.

Questions about Raines's management style—his penchant for giving preferential treatment to favored stars, his celebrated fondness for "flooding the zone" on big stories, severely stretching resources—weren't addressed at all. Indeed, more than one *Times* staffer pointed out that the paper's national staff would not have been in need of the services of an untested young reporter with a spotty track record had a number of veterans not been pushed out by Raines last year.

Of course, plagiarism, and even outright fraud, can occur at any news organization, and certainly the lion's share of the blame for this scandal should fall on Blair. As commentators have noted, the normal journalistic checks and balances are put in place with the assumption that everyone—reporters, editors and readers—shares an interest in getting to the truth. "The person who did this is Jayson Blair," *Times* publisher Arthur Sulzberger Jr. said in Sunday's story. "Let's not begin to demonize our executives." As the *Times* seeks to come to grips with how this could have happened, there is bound to be a lot more soul-searching in the months ahead.

The News NOT Fit to Print

BY KAREN YOURISH
NEWSWEEK, MAY 26, 2003

Jayson Blair isn't the first journalist to deceive readers—and he probably won't be the last. It's no wonder, than, that the profession is struggling with a credibility problem. A brief walk down the Hall of Shame:

YELLOW JOURNALISM, 1890s: Dueling New York publishers Joseph Pulitzer and William Randolph Hearst sensationalize and manufacture events to sell millions of papers.

STALINIST STOOGE?, 1930s: Walter Duranty, the *New York Times* Soviet correspondent, ignores the brutality of Stalin's regime, telling readers at one point that no one in Ukraine is starving when, in fact, millions were dying.

BLOOD BROS., 1964: The *Times* runs a series about a 400-member Harlem gang called the Blood Brothers who were said to be "trained to maim and kill" white people. It's denounced as wildly exaggerated, and the *Times* admits years later that the story was "hyperbole to a high degree."

RED CHINA, 1972: The *San Francisco Examiner* publishes a series on reporter Bob Patterson's undercover travels in China, but learns afterward that Patterson had never left his Hong Kong hotel room.

BOOGIE DOWN, 1976: *New York* magazine wows America with the supposedly true story of a Brooklyn disco dancer named Vincent, who serves as the inspiration for John Travolta's hip-swiveling character in the hit movie *Saturday Night Fever.* In 1997, however, the writer, Nik Cohn, admits to having fabricated the article.

JIMMY'S WORLD, 1980: *Washington Post* reporter Janet Cooke writes a heartbreaking account about an 8-year-old heroin addict for which she wins a Pulitzer the following year. Two days after receiving the award, Cooke admits "Jimmy" doesn't exist.

ADOLF'S TELL-ALL, 1983: In late April, the German magazine *Stern* announces its acquisition of Hitler's diaries and publishes excerpts. London's *Sunday Times, Newsweek* and others cover the find before discovering in early May that the diaries are a complete hoax.

TRADING INSIDE, 1985: *Wall Street Journal* reporter R. Foster Winans is convicted of securities fraud for using info he knew would appear in the *WSJ* the next day to make money on the stock market. Winans had written the popular "Heard on the Street" column that analysts believed could cause stocks to rise and fall.

TRUE COLORS, 1997: *Newsweek's* editor, the late Maynard Parker, comes under fire for publishing items speculating on the author of the book *Primary Colors*, when he knew it was written by Joe Klein, then one of his own reporters.

THE YOUNG AND RESTLESS, 1998: Stephen Glass, a 25-year-old writer at *The New Republic*, is fired after his editors find he had fabricated all or parts of 27 of the 41 articles he'd written for the magazine. A few years earlier, Ruth Shalit, another brash young *TNR* writer, admitted to plagiarizing passages and fabricating facts.

BOSTON BLUES, 1998: Columnist Mike Barnicle resigns from the *Boston Globe* amid allegations he had made up sources and facts and stolen material from other writers. Two months earlier another *Globe* columnist, Patricia Smith, was fired for making up characters and dialogue.

NOT SO SMART, 2003: Two reporters from the *Salt Lake Tribune* are fired after splitting $20,000 from the *National Enquirer* for help on a July 2, 2002, story that alleged Elizabeth Smart's family was involved in a sex ring. The tabloid has since retracted the story.

The *Boston Globe* Media Column[6]

BY MARK JURKOWITZ
THE BOSTON GLOBE, MAY 28, 2003

If the initial responses from news executives are any indication, one byproduct of the stunning Jayson Blair scandal may be a tightening of the editing process at newspapers around the country. "Editors need to sort of prosecute stories" and be more aggressive, said the *Des Moines Register*'s editor, Paul Anger. "They need to find holes. We've sort of reminded ourselves of this."

Bob Steele, ethics director at the Poynter Institute, a media think tank, uses a similar term—"prosecutorial editing"—to describe a more hands-on role for editors who must ask "very hard questions, meaningful questions" of their reporters.

This effort to focus on more rigorous standards follows the furor triggered by Blair, the *New York Times* staff member who resigned after allegations of plagiarism and fabrication. The scandal plunged the nation's most prestigious daily—and to some extent the entire newspaper industry—into a crisis of credibility.

At the *Plain Dealer* of Cleveland, editor Douglas Clifton said staff members had asked themselves: " 'Could that happen here?' The answer was yes; I think it could happen anywhere."

Anger added: "I think all of journalism is embarrassed."

The industry response to the Blair scandal has run the gamut from schadenfreude to overreaction to efforts at reform.

The *St. Paul Pioneer Press* and the *Plain Dealer* will soon begin sending letters asking people who have been written about in their pages if they had been covered accurately. The *Boston Globe* plans to increase monitoring of, and accountability for, errors. The *Sun* of Baltimore is talking about creating an ombudsman's column. The *Oregonian*, in Portland, is discussing whether its newsroom is receptive enough to internal criticism.

The American Society of Newspaper Editors plans to investigate whether college journalism students are given a sufficiently solid ethics education. And staff members from the Poynter Institute will begin traveling around the country to conduct one-day ethics workshops.

While the industry grapevine speculates about the fate of the *New York Times*'s executive editor, Howell Raines, the paper has announced a series of steps—including the hiring of 20 new staff

6. Republished with permission of *The Boston Globe*, from "The *Boston Globe* Media Column," May 28, 2003; permission conveyed through Copyright Clearance Center, Inc.

members, decentralized decision-making, and the creation of a committee to recommend improvements in the newsroom culture and organization—to address issues raised by the Blair crisis.

In another development yesterday, the *Washington Post* reported that Rick Bragg, a high-profile reporter for the *Times* who was suspended after revelations last week that much of the on-scene reporting for a 2002 article under his byline had been done by another journalist, plans to leave the paper. A *Times* spokeswoman, contacted yesterday, did not confirm that Bragg intended to quit.

In some quarters, the *Times's* travails were cause for both scathing sarcasm and suggestions for Draconian remedies. Some fans of a popular media website submitted limericks assailing Blair's mental state and work habits. On a more serious note, the magazine *Editor & Publisher* published an editorial calling the use of anonymous sources "the crack cocaine of journalism." The founder of *USA Today*, Al Neuharth, went a step further, writing that the "only sure way to separate fact from fiction is to ban all anonymous sources."

In some newsrooms, the episode triggered almost immediate scrutiny of practices and procedures. *Oregonian* editor Sandra Mims Rowe sent a memo to the staff kicking off a discussion of issues, ranging from anonymous sources to communication skills among editors. "We used [the Blair problem] as a case study," she said.

At the *Sun*, editor Bill Marimow and assistant managing editor for projects Rebecca Corbett convened a seminar to solicit ideas for strengthening the newspaper's commitment to accuracy and accountability.

St. Paul Pioneer Press editor Vicki Gowler reviewed policies for evaluating interns and staff members with senior editors and wrote a column instructing readers on how they can communicate concerns to the paper.

The *Globe*—where Blair worked as an intern and a stringer in the late 1990s and was found, on some occasions, to have committed errors and ethical lapses—is reinforcing policies concerning everything from anonymous sources to tracking errors. "A more rigorous monitoring system within our newsroom is highly likely," said editor Martin Baron. (The *Washington Post* and the *Chicago Tribune* did not return calls seeking comment on steps they might be taking as a result of the *Times* revelations.)

Of course, no one can be sure that this tidal wave of buzz and backlash from the Blair episode will ultimately translate into more solid journalism.

"Within the industry, we have a tendency to wring our hands after a Jayson Blair . . . and then go to a conference to talk about how we can do this better," said Robert Leger, president of the Society of Professional Journalists, suggesting that the news business sometimes seems to favor introspection over real change.

Project for Excellence in Journalism director Tom Rosenstiel said that in the wake of this scandal, media outlets are now scrambling to provide a clean bill of health to their consumers—in effect to "demonstrate to my public that we have stricter standards than they think I do."

A Plague of Plagiarism[7]

BY MARK FITZGERALD
THE WRITER, JULY 2002

Stephen E. Ambrose, Louis W. Roberts, Doris Kearns Goodwin, the Rev. Edward Mullins and John L. Casti never would have suffered such public opprobrium if only they had learned from Dave Barry. Now what, you might ask, could a syndicated columnist whose only place in the pantheon of literature is as the undisputed king of booger jokes possibly teach such eminent figures as, respectively, the bestselling chronicler of World War II; the editor and translator of *Sources for the History of Cyprus, Vol. VIII: Latin Texts from the First Century* B.C. *to the Seventeenth Century* A.D.; the Pulitzer Prize–winning presidential historian; the Episcopalian rector of Christ Church Cranbrook, located in Bloomfield Hills, Mich.; and, finally, the author of *Mathematical Mountaintops: The Five Most Famous Problems of All Times*?

Simple: Dave Barry always scrupulously attributes the source of any true fact that wanders into his column. As we now know, the other writers listed above are, shall we say, less inclined to give credit where credit is due. When Dave Barry comments on, for example, an exploding commode, he not only names the newspaper that published the incident, but also the reporter who wrote the article—and even the "alert reader" who passed it along.

It's a long-standing principle that any material borrowed in writing must be fully attributed to its original author. Yet episodes of plagiarism, that most slippery and discomfiting of literary crimes, have a way of confusing our thinking about even the most straightforward of ethical boundaries. That's especially true of the spate of plagiarism that emerged earlier this year.

How could Ambrose, who celebrated World War II bomber pilots in *The Wild Blue*, or Goodwin, who vividly captured the triumphs and tragedies of *The Fitzgeralds and the Kennedys*, be among the bad guys?

Yet they were not the only solid citizens standing in a lineup accused of literary theft. Louis W. Roberts, who was at the time the chairman of the classics department of the State University of New York at Albany, is accused of plagiarizing translations of centuries-old Latin texts. The Rev. Edward Mullins allegedly copied entire sermons and church bulletin articles from Internet sites. Science writer John L. Casti acknowledged carrying out perhaps the

7. Article by Mark Fitzgerald from *The Writer* July 2002. Copyright © Mark Fitzgerald. Reprinted with permission.

most improbable plagiarism: He copied math—not the answers, but the explanations of problems he included in his book on history's famous mathematical stumpers.

As usual in plagiarism cases, the authors offered initial explanations that they had merely been sloppy with notes and neglected to attribute one or two sentences. But as Thomas Mallon writes in his invaluable exploration of plagiarism, *Stolen Words*, text theft is a serial crime: Plagiarism, he says, "is something people may do for a variety of reasons but almost always something they do more than once." So it was this time around. Critics found that Ambrose had lifted material in five other works. Goodwin ended up acknowledging that *The Fitzgeralds and the Kennedys* included scores of quotations or close paraphrases that were not attributed to their original authors.

Still, if professional writers with several bestsellers under their belt can run afoul of the line between attribution and theft, is there any hope for the rest of us?

It turns out that nonfiction and history writers, working in isolation from each other, have adopted remarkably similar habits to

> ***Plagiarism . . . "is something people may do for a variety of reasons but almost always something they do more than once."***
> **—Thomas Mallon, author**

avoid falling into or near the swamp of plagiarism. "There are no courses on this. As an historian, no one trains you on it. You just kind of learn by the seat of your pants," says Donald L. Miller, most recently the author, with the late Henry Steele Commager, of *The Story of World War II*.

What follows, then, are some of the principles, warnings, tips and techniques writers use to ensure they don't stray from research to cribbing:

Beware of well-trod ground. Other historians aren't surprised that Goodwin stumbled when writing about the Kennedys, a family that's launched a thousand previous books. "When you write about the Kennedys or the Roosevelts, you've got to rely on other books and secondary sources—and secondary sources will get you into trouble," says Steve Neal, a *Chicago Sun-Times* columnist whose most recent book was *Harry and Ike: The Partnership That Remade the Postwar World*.

Neal once withdrew from a Doubleday book contract to write about Woodrow Wilson because he believed others had already captured the subject. Instead, he wrote a biography of Wendell L. Willkie. "My view is, if a subject has been done before, there's no reason for me to do a book on it," Neal says.

In *The Wrong Man: The Final Verdict in the Dr. Sam Sheppard Murder Case*, James Neff wrote about the most intensely covered crime and trial of the 1950s. Yet the paucity of good writing about the case, he says, ensured that he wasn't even tempted to lift material.

Beware of secondary sources. It's a point that bears repeating, says Miller: "One little trick that writers get into with secondary sources is they'll like something in a book, so they'll use it and go down to the footnote and cite the same source. So you're depending on that guy to be correct, which isn't always the case. Unless you go to the primary sources, you are in for the headache of your life."

Good nonfiction and history writing takes time. With his staff of researchers, Stephen E. Ambrose has become a writing factory, churning out an average of more than a book a year since the mid-1990s. That's simply too fast, other writers say.

"My first book took a long time; the [second] book took a long time. The Sheppard book took forever," says Neff, who is investigations editor at the *Seattle Times*. "If you're working too quickly, that's when the sloppiness and inaccuracies creep in." Adds Neal: "David McCullough took 10 years to write *John Adams*. Robert Caro took decades writing about [Lyndon] Johnson. To do a good history takes time."

***"Unless you go to the primary sources, you are in for the headache of your life."*— Donald Miller, author**

Keep an orderly filing system. These days, the most common plea of writers found plagiarizing is that they mixed up their own writing with notes downloaded on their computer. So it was kind of refreshing that Goodwin blamed her problems on her system of making handwritten notes on index cards.

Both systems are flawed, says Miller, who adds that many writers seem confused about how best to keep files. "Whenever I'm at a reading or a book signing, if there are writers in the audience, invariably they want to know about your filing system," he says.

As it happens, Miller and Neff share a common habit: Rather than write notes from source material on paper or computer, they insist on photocopying the document. That way they can never confuse the material with their own writing.

"If you use research assistants you have to demand the actual [photocopied] page because you can't rely on their notes," Miller says. Writers need not store a mountain of paper, he adds: "Sometimes I'll just cut out a paragraph from the Xerox [photocopy] that I want and put the citation right there on it."

Always attribute—and always attribute as you go along. Miller's 1996 book, *City of the Century: The Epic of Chicago and the Making of America*, is peppered with contemporary quotes from people of all walks who were rebuilding Chicago after the Great Fire. Those quotations are the result of hard work. "You try to get the best source available. I may look at a dozen sources, because I tend to over-research my books, and . . . you learn after awhile who are the reliable eyes with which to look at the story. Then I go searching for the compelling [contemporary] prose that nails it," he says.

Neff worked in a similar way on the Sheppard book, weaving a "you are there" narrative by consulting photos, newsreels and the trial transcript, then punctuating the story with contemporary quotes. He made especially good use of the vivid newspaper reporting of the so-called "sob sisters" of the 1950s, such as the *New York Journal-American*'s Dorothy Kilgallen.

To ensure accurate attribution, both Neff and Miller write their footnotes while they work on each chapter, rather than wait till the entire book is written.

Finally, check, re-check and check again. When Miller finished *The Story of World War II*, seven student assistants—"that's 14 eyes"—spent four months fact-checking the book even before Simon & Schuster's copy editors went to work on it. Miller himself went back to every document or book he had consulted to check every quote. "I know a lot of historians who do the same thing," he says. "After all, as historians, we're supposed to be in the veracity business."

While they require hard work, these techniques are simple and straightforward. The damage when a bestselling author ignores them extends beyond just that writer's work, says Steve Neal. "I do think [Ambrose's] reputation has been seriously tarnished," he says. "That's a shame because when narrative history is popular, that's good. For all writers."

When Pastors Plagiarize[8]

CHRISTIANITY TODAY, DECEMBER 9, 2002

A friend of this magazine tells a disturbing story: While traveling on business, he visits a local church. He finds himself listening to a finely crafted, well illustrated, and moving sermon, but feels as if he has heard it before. When he returns home, he opens a Max Lucado book and discovers that the sermon was a recitation of one chapter. The pastor had not acknowledged his debt in either the sermon or the worship bulletin.

Unfortunately, whether it's stealing from homiletic giants or anonymous Internet sermon services, the problem is with us. Many pastors plagiarize. These are good men and women who otherwise are models of probity. What gives when it comes to preaching? What gives is that we find ourselves in three unhealthy situations.

First, we live in a media-saturated age in which we can watch, listen to, or read the brightest and best preachers at any time. The pressure on the local pastor to match this eloquence is felt on both sides of the pulpit.

Second, the pastor is expected to do what no other public communicator is asked to do. Depending on the tradition, the pastor preaches and teaches original material, one to four times a week, for anywhere from 15 minutes to an hour. Commentators on NPR and CBS have maybe three or four one-minute commentaries to write each week. *Newsweek* columnists generally write 700 words every other week. Politicians may give more speeches per week, but the content is canned and composed by a staff.

Third, the pastor is about the only public communicator today whose efforts are not collaborative or edited by others before they are made public. We in the church still suffer from the romantic illusion (a result of the European Enlightenment and American rugged individualism) that the sermon is the creative, prophetic effort of the lonely individual who wrestles with the text in a closed study and emerges with a revelation from God. This is silly. During many eras, in the English Reformation for example, sermons were crafted by church leaders, printed, and distributed to parishes, where local pastors would preach them word for word. Congregations did not blink. It was assumed that sermons were not individualistic efforts but the work of the church.

To be sure, such sermons were not the most vital instruments of renewal, precisely because they contained nothing personal and immediate. So it remains right for pastors to prepare a particular

8. Used by permission, *Christianity Today*, 2002.

word for their very local congregations. But congregations are unfair to pastors, and pastors are unfair to their congregations, if everyone assumes that every idea, illustration, and outline the pastor uses should be original.

The solution is simple. Congregations should allow, even encourage, their pastors to use the best material from books, magazines, and the Internet. Pastors who rely on these sources are not lazy, inept, or irresponsible. Pastors, for their part, should always credit their sources.

Naturally, there are gray areas, and to credit every illustration or quote would clutter the sermon or worship bulletin (pastors and church boards may wish to download and discuss specific guidelines from PreachingToday.com: *www.christianitytoday.com/go/sermonguide*). But if a pastor reads a dynamite sermon that fits a congregation's needs, we see no reason not to say, "I found this wonderful sermon by Max Lucado that I thought you should hear. Let me preach it to you as best I can."

III. Copyrights

Editor's Introduction

As many writers, poets, musicians, and movie directors are learning the hard way, it is very easy in today's high-tech world for people to gain access to works and ideas and use them for personal gain without a thought to compensating their creators. While the courts and policy makers are trying to come up with a solution to this problem, the only sure way to protect one's work is to take matters into one's own hands by obtaining a copyright. As defined by *Microsoft Encarta*, copyright is a "branch of law granting authors the exclusive privilege to reproduce, distribute, perform, or display their creative works. The goal of copyright law is to encourage authors to invest effort in creating new works of art and literature. . . . Copyright only protects the words, notes, or images that the creator has used. It does not protect any ideas or concepts revealed by the work." Chapter 3 deals exclusively with the difficult issues surrounding copyrights today. It covers laws passed that protect and extend copyrights, as well as legal battles over them.

The first article in this chapter, entitled "The Digital Millennium Copyright Act," examines the newest legislation passed to amend U.S. copyright law. Edward H. Freeman explores some of the history behind the Digital Millennium Copyright Act (DMCA), who supports it, who objects to it, and the ins and outs of the act itself. Freeman also examines the case of *United States v. ElcomSoft Ltd.,* brought against an alleged violator of the DMCA. It involved Adobe's accusation that the Russian programmer Dmitry Sklyarov and his employer, software producer ElcomSoft Ltd., developed and sold software to skirt security measures that protected Adobe's eBooks from being copied, printed, and sent illegally to other users. Freeman looks at the details of this case and its effect on the publishing world. An accompanying sidebar discusses protecting copyrights internationally.

The second article looks at the Digital Millennium Copyright Act (DMCA) in more depth. "Congress Protects Copyrights on the Web," by Tony Case, focuses mainly on the newspaper industry and on how the passage of the DMCA has granted newspapers greater protection against piracy. The article also examines the role Congress has taken in passing laws related to intellectual property in light of IP's growing importance to creative people in various industries and professions.

The next article, "Supreme Court Upholds Extended Copyrights," discusses another court case that generated a hailstorm of controversy and the law it was challenging. With many copyrighted materials on the brink of being transferred into the public domain, Congress passed the Sonny Bono Copyright Extension Act, which extended copyrights by 20 years. Opponents voiced their concern, and the Supreme Court soon found itself embroiled in the controversy when *Eldred v. Ashcroft* was brought before it. This article looks at the Supreme Court's ruling in *Eldred v. Ashcroft* and the effect—if any—it has had on the copyright extension.

Jeff Belle further examines the *Eldred v. Ashcroft* case in "Broken Links and Broken Laws," where he also considers a different copyright controversy caused by Dan Wallach and his Dilbert Hack Page. Belle looks at the trouble in which Wallach found himself after creating a Web page dedicated to the cartoon Dilbert, and he reviews Wallach's arguments for the legality of the URL and the result of the dispute. In citing this case alongside *Eldred*, Belle explores the ever-present problems with copyright laws and why the ambiguities in the laws must be resolved. In an accompanying sidebar, Tyra W. Hilliard reiterates the importance of copyrights and discusses who owns the rights to works created.

The last three articles in this chapter discuss writers' and poets' struggles with preventing online copyright infringement of their work. In the first article, "Copyright on the Web," Emily A. Vander Veer discusses what the U.S. Copyright Office refers to as "decentralized infringement"—an exchange of copyrighted materials over the Web without the copyright holder's permission. She describes the two different places work might appear: a site the copyright holder never heard of and/or an archived database. Since presenting work at either site is illegal if permission has not been granted, Vander Veer also presents nine ways writers might protect their rights and prevent this from happening to them

In the next article, "Poetic License: What Every Poet Should Know About Copyright," Tonya Marie Evans discusses the direct relation of copyrights to writers and poets. In light of the ambiguities in the term "copyright," she tries to explain to writers what copyrights are. She begins by defining a copyright and then goes on to differentiate copyrights from patents and trademarks. She also discusses the "mail myth," how to obtain a copyright, and why obtaining a copyright is advisable for poets. Instructions on registering copyrights at the Copyright Office are provided in a sidebar at the end of the article.

The final article in this chapter, "Who Owns History?," deals with the problem freelance writers have had asserting their rights, and the court case that confronted the issue head-on. *Tasini et al. v. The New York Times et al.* was a landmark ruling in favor of freelance writers. Challenging some of the most prestigious newspapers in the country, *Tasini* sought to remove freelance writers' work from online publications and databases that had the right to present the articles in print but not electronically. Jason Williams examines the *Tasini* case, the legal issues surrounding it, the outcome, and the long-term ramifications of the decision.

The Digital Millennium Copyright Act[1]

BY EDWARD H. FREEMAN
INFORMATION SYSTEMS SECURITY, SEPTEMBER/OCTOBER 2002

On October 12, 1998, the U.S. Congress passed the controversial Digital Millennium Copyright Act (DMCA), ending many months of negotiations. President Clinton signed the Act into law on October 28. The DMCA made major changes in U.S. copyright law to address new issues created by the Internet and other new technologies. The Act also amended U.S. copyright law to comply with the World Intellectual Property Organization (WIPO) Copyright Treaty adopted at the WIPO Diplomatic Conference in December 1996.

The recording industry and the large software companies greeted DMCA with great enthusiasm and lobbied diligently for its passage. Civil libertarians, small software developers and hackers were equally opposed to the Act's restrictions on their activities. It was inevitable that there would be a major battle between the two sides of this issue.

This column deals with Dmitry Sklyarov, a young Russian graduate student and programmer who was arrested in 2001 for violating the terms of the DMCA. Sklyarov's employer, a Russian software firm called ElcomSoft, had offered a software program that could circumvent technological protections on copyrighted software. The reaction to Sklyarov's arrest is indicative of a lengthy disagreement between different segments of the computer industry.

Copyright Protection

The Copyright Clause of the U.S. Constitution empowers Congress to "promote the Progress of Science and useful Arts, by securing for limited Times to Authors and Inventors the exclusive Right to their Writings and Discoveries."[1] Courts have traditionally held that the intellectual property law is designed primarily to encourage the creation of new works and technologies. Compensation for creators has always been a secondary consideration, primarily to encourage innovators to continue their work.

---

1. Article by Edward H. Freeman from *Information Systems Security* 11:4 (4–8) (September/October 2002). Copyright © 2002 CRC Press LLC. Reprinted with permission.

In a series of acts passed as early as 1790, Congress has always regulated and upgraded copyright protection. The courts have traditionally agreed that the words "authors" and "writings" are to be interpreted to mean more than just printed materials. Consequently, almost any media (e.g., computer programs, photographs, sculpture, choreography, and musical recordings) can be copyrighted. The Copyright Revision Act of 1976[2] included computer software and databases as literary works protected by federal copyright law and eligible for copyright protection.

Copyright laws protect only the tangible expression of an idea.

Copyright laws protect only the tangible expression of an idea. Ideas, concepts, principles, discoveries, procedures, and systems do not qualify for copyright protection, although they may be protected as trade secrets or patents. This distinction can be unclear and has led to a great deal of copyright litigation.

In an 1879 case,[3] the U.S. Supreme Court illustrated the effect of this distinction. A copyrighted book outlined a new double-entry bookkeeping system. The book detailed how the system worked and contained printed forms that could be used to implement the new system. Another author published a different set of forms, which accomplished the same purpose.

The U.S. Supreme Court held that the first author's copyright did not provide an exclusive right to make and use all bookkeeping forms based on the ideas expressed in the book. Only those forms that were actually a part of the book could be copyrighted. The ideas of the bookkeeping system could not be protected, only the actual forms used to implement the system. In a more recent case, the court held that sweepstakes instructions could not be copyrighted because such instructions can only be expressed in a limited number of ways and the idea merges with the expression.[4]

Copyright law does not give copyright holders absolute control over their works. A major limitation is the *fair use* doctrine. Fair use allows individuals to make a copy of a work for personal use or for education, commentary, criticism, parody, or other socially beneficial use. As an example of the doctrine, a book critic may write a negative review of a copyrighted book and quote brief sections from the book, even if the author does not approve of the column.

Courts will use the following four major factors to see if an action is allowed under the fair use doctrine:

1. *The purpose and character of the use.* Courts are more likely to find fair use where the use is for noncommercial purposes rather than commercial.

2. *The nature of the copyrighted work.* A particular use is more likely to be fair use when the copied work is factual rather than creative.
3. *The amount and substantiality of the portion used in relation to the copyrighted work as a whole.* A court will balance this factor toward a finding of fair use where the amount taken is small or insignificant in proportion to the overall work.
4. T*he effect of the use upon the potential market for or value of the copyrighted work.* If the court finds the newly created work is not a substitute product for the copyrighted work, it will more likely weigh this factor in favor of fair use.[5]

The Digital Millennium Copyright Act

The Digital Millennium Copyright Act was enacted in 1998. The Act inserted new laws into the copyright statutes to discourage copying of copyrighted materials. In particular, the DMCA added new *anti-circumvention* provisions. These provisions prohibited gaining unauthorized access to a work by "circumventing a technological protection measure" put in place by the copyright owner where such protection measure otherwise effectively controls access to a copyrighted work.[6]

There are seven exemptions built into the DMCA. These permit the circumvention of access and copy controls for limited purposes and the limited distribution of circumvention tools in particular circumstances. These seven exemptions are for:

1. Libraries, archives, and educational institutions for acquisition purposes
2. Law enforcement and intelligence-gathering activities
3. Reverse-engineering in order to develop interoperable programs
4. Encryption research
5. Protecting minors from material on the Internet
6. Protecting the privacy of personally identifying information
7. Security testing

In addition to these seven exemptions, the Library of Congress must submit a report every three years that will define those measures that prevent the "fair use" of copyrighted works. The DMCA also contains provisions that ensure that the traditional rights of copyright law still apply to the DMCA. The rights, remedies, limitations, or defenses to claims of copyright infringement still apply. The DMCA also states that these provisions should not affect the rights to free speech or freedom of the press for activities using electronics, telecommunications, or computing products.

International Copyright

There is no such thing as an "international copyright" that will automatically protect an author's writings throughout the world. Protection against unauthorized use in a particular country basically depends on the national laws of that country. However, most countries offer protection to foreign works under certain conditions which have been greatly simplified by international copyright treaties and conventions. There are two principal international copyright conventions, the Berne Union for the Protection of Literary and Artistic Property (Berne Convention) and the Universal Copyright Convention (UCC).

The United States became a member of the Berne Convention on March 1, 1989. It has been a member of the UCC since September 16, 1955. Generally, the works of an author who is a national or domiciliary of a country that is a member of these treaties or works first published in a member country or published within 30 days of first publication in a Berne Union country may claim protection under them. There are no formal requirements in the Berne Convention. Under the UCC, any formality in a national law may be satisfied by the use of a notice of copyright in the form and position specified in the UCC. A UCC notice should consist of the symbol © (C in a circle) accompanied by the year of first publication and the name of the copyright proprietor (example: © 1995 John Doe). This notice must be placed in such manner and location as to give reasonable notice of the claim to copyright. Since the Berne Convention prohibits formal requirements that affect the "exercise and enjoyment" of the copyright, the United States changed its law on March 1, 1989, to make the use of a copyright notice optional. U.S. law, however, still provides certain advantages for use of a copyright notice; for example, the use of a copyright notice can defeat a defense of "innocent infringement."

Even if the work cannot be brought under an international convention, protection may be available in other countries by virtue of a bilateral agreement between the U.S. and other countries or under specific provision of a country's national laws. (See generally Circular 38a International Copyright Relations of the United States.)

An author who wishes copyright protection for his or her work in a particular country should first determine the extent of protection available to works of foreign authors in that country. If possible, this should be done before the work is published anywhere, because protection may depend on the facts existing at the time of first publication.

There are some countries that offer little or no copyright protection to any foreign works. For current information on the requirements and protection provided by other countries, it may be advisable to consult an expert familiar with foreign copyright laws. The U.S. Copyright Office is not permitted to recommend agents or attorneys or to give legal advice on foreign laws.

Source: Library of Congress, Copyright Office, FL-100, June 1999

Other sections of the DMCA prohibit the manufacture, import, or traffic of tools that are designed to enable another to circumvent protection to copy a protected work. The DMCA provides for both civil and criminal penalties carrying a maximum of five years' imprisonment and/or a fine of up to $500,000 for a first offense.

Facts of the Case

According to its Web site, Adobe Systems Incorporated is the second largest PC software company in the United States, with annual revenues exceeding $1 billion. The company is headquartered in San Jose, California, and employs more than 2900 people worldwide. Adobe's best-known products are Acrobat and PhotoShop.[7]

Electronic book technology (eBook) allows a user to download the text of a book via the Internet. The Adobe Acrobat eBook Reader enables users to read eBooks on their own computers with no special hardware. The free software package displays pictures and graphics similar to those found in printed books. Authors and publishers must purchase the Adobe package to make their works available to interested readers, but anybody can download the eBook Reader at no charge. In most cases, publishers charge a user before releasing the eBook to him.

Adobe's eBook Reader allows users to make some fair use of eBooks, at a level of permission selected by the publisher. Users can copy, loan, or print Adobe-format eBooks only if the publisher sets these permissions to allow this use. If a user's hard drive crashes, he can contact Adobe to get a duplicate copy of the eBook. The eBook Reader does not permit making copies for personal use or loaning the eBook to a friend unless the publisher authorizes these actions. Under the fair use doctrine, such rights are legal for books in paper format.

ElcomSoft is a privately owned software development company headquartered in Moscow. Established in 1990, ElcomSoft specializes in producing Windows productivity and utility applications for businesses and individuals. ElcomSoft has developed various security-related products, including password products used by the U.S. Government to recover Word and Quicken files when the password has been lost or forgotten.[8]

One of ElcomSoft's products is the Advanced eBook Processor (AEBPR). AEBPR removes the technological protection from Adobe's eBooks and converts them into Adobe's PDF format.[9] This allows eBooks to be read or processed by third-party software, not just by Adobe's eBook Reader. AEBPR removes the various restrictions against copying and printing eBooks that publishers can enable or disable under the Adobe system. Using AEBPR, eBook purchasers can:

- Transport eBooks from one computer to another
- Make a backup copy as a protection against hard disk failure
- Copy and paste parts of an eBook to another document
- Print sections of eBooks

- Allow usage on alternate operating systems, such as Linux or PDAs (Adobe's format works only on Macs and Microsoft Windows PCs)

Dmitry Sklyarov is a young Russian programmer, a Ph.D. student at Moscow University, and an employee of ElcomSoft. In July 2001, he was invited to speak at DEF CON, a major annual technical conference in Las Vegas. DEF CON is widely attended by professional and amateur security experts and hackers. Its Web page (*www.defcon.org*) describes the conference as "the largest hacker convention on the planet!" Sklyarov's presentation concerned weaknesses in Adobe's eBook technology software.

Sklyarov was arrested as he was leaving Las Vegas to return to Moscow. ElcomSoft and Sklyarov were both charged with violation of the DMCA. The charges were criminal rather than civil, and were based on allegations from Adobe that ElcomSoft was distributing the key that unlocked the copyright protection for Adobe eBook files. They were charged with "making available" circumvention technology and for "aiding and abetting." Sklyarov spent approximately three weeks in jail, until he was released on $50,000 bond.

Extensive meetings with the nonprofit Electronic Frontier Foundation—and widespread protests on the Internet—occurred. Adobe soon announced that it did not consider the prosecution of Sklyarov in the best interests of the parties involved or of the industry. Nevertheless, the U.S. Justice Department continued the prosecution. On August 28, Sklyarov was brought into court in handcuffs and indicted by a grand jury. On December 13, he was released from U.S. custody and allowed to return to Russia.

ElcomSoft filed motions with the court to dismiss the charges, claiming that the DMCA was overly vague, violated constitutional guarantees to free speech, and infringed the established right to fair use of copyrighted materials. On May 8, 2002, U.S. District Court Judge Ronald Whyte denied ElcomSoft's motion to dismiss the charges.

"The DMCA does not eliminate fair use or substantially impair the fair use rights of anyone," the judge wrote in a 35-page opinion. "The fair user may find it more difficult to engage in certain fair uses with regards to electronic books, but nevertheless, fair use is still available."[10] Even if the circumvention software allows the user to copy sections in conformance with "fair usage," the software still violated the terms of the DMCA. The judge also ruled that the DMCA was neither vague nor did it violate the First Amendment. This ruling allows the criminal prosecution and trial to continue in the courts. A trial date for the case will be set later in 2002.

Analysis

Civil libertarians and organizations involved with electronic freedom expressed outrage at Sklyarov's arrest. The incident provoked headlines, protest, and controversy throughout the world. The hacker community was particularly outraged. Numerous Web sites with names such as *www.freedmitry.org* and *www.boycottadobe.com* (complete with pictures of Sklyarov's wife and children in Moscow) quickly sprang up to increase public awareness and to raise funds for legal fees.

Many legal analysts were strongly opposed to Sklyarov's arrest. Professor Michael Landau of Georgia State University wrote:

> Granted, certain measures are needed in order to stop widespread piracy of copyrighted material. Certain measures are also needed to prevent unauthorized access to confidential and password-protected files. However, a balance must be established that also allows encryption research, and the distribution of information and/or software that allows certain copying by authorized users.
>
> It should not be illegal to copy an excerpt of a book that the user owns. It should not be illegal for the owner of a legitimate authorized copy to make a second copy for a second e-book reader or laptop computer.
>
> Not all "circumvention of technological measures" are objectionable. I am hopeful that the courts, and if necessary Congress, will realize this in the future.[11]

The Business Software Alliance (*www.bsa.org*), an industry group, of course, had a different viewpoint. In an August 30 press release, they wrote:

> The DMCA was designed to promote a safe and legal online world while advancing the dynamic change that is synonymous with the Internet. Since the DMCA's enactment the evidence of the abundance of creative content available online is proof that the DMCA is working. . . . The DMCA is an effective law, which has enabled the Internet to prosper through both the distribution of content and the correct digital rights to protect such material.

Adobe also distributed a press release that defended its position in the controversy:

> Adobe designed the Acrobat eBook Reader for Windows to allow users to exchange eBooks like printed books. The Acrobat eBook Reader does allow customers to move the eBooks they purchase between computers through its lending and giving features. If the publishers enable these features, the buyer of an eBook can loan or transfer to another Acrobat eBook Reader on the network.
>
> Lending, printing, copying and text-to-speech are permissions enabled by the publisher. The ElcomSoft software product violates the permissions set by the publisher to protect the copyrighted works of artists, authors, and publishers, making the copyrighted content available for unlimited duplication and distribution. Keep in mind that the eBook market is an emerging one. Adobe and its partners are always exploring new ways to protect copyrights and allow for fair use.

Conclusion

The Sklyarov arrest resolved none of the inherent problems of DMCA. Pictures of a young Russian citizen being led into court in handcuffs did nothing to resolve some of the very legitimate concerns of the software and recording industries. Further clarification of anti-circumvention laws, along with serious discussions of the outstanding issues between the different interest groups, will help prevent further such incidents.

Notes

1. Art I, § 8, cl8.
2. Public Law 94-553 (October 19, 1976).
3. *Baker v. Selden,* 101 US 99.
4. *Morrissey v. Proctor & Gamble Co.*, 379 F.2d 675 (1st Cir. 1967).
5. 17 U.S.C. § 107(1–4).
6. 17 U.S.C. § 1201(a)(1)(1998).
7. Further information about Adobe can be found at *www.adobe.com.*
8. Further information about ElcomSoft can be found at *www.elcomsoft.com.*
9. AEBPR is no longer available in the United States.
10. "Judge says Russia software company can be tried," *www.reuters.com*, posted on May 8, 2002.
11. Michael Landau, "The DMCA's Chilling Effect on Encryption Research," *www.Gigalaw.com.*

Congress Protects Copyrights on the Web[2]

BY TONY CASE
EDITOR & PUBLISHER, DECEMBER 12, 1998

Praising a new law designed to strengthen copyright protections in cyberspace, newspaper lawyers say it clarifies safeguards in the new medium.

The Digital Millennium Copyright Act, which became law in October and was among hundreds of Internet-related bills introduced in Congress this year, gives traditional and software publishers, along with other creators of online material, greater ammunition against pirates who reproduce information without permission.

The law also shields online service providers and telephone companies from liability when customers transmit or post copyrighted data, provided the service providers take prompt action against offenders once alerted.

The law affirms that the standard of "fair use," which allows for noncommercial copying of copyrighted material, such as a news story about a newsworthy book, carries into the online realm.

In addition, it prohibits the circumvention of encryption technologies and other means of protecting digital data.

And to further global copyright standards, the law implements two international digital-information treaties ratified two years ago by the United Nations World Intellectual Property Organization (WIPO), which works to guarantee copyright protections across borders.

"This is not necessarily a change in the copyright law, which is very strong to begin with. But now if someone circumvents the copyright protections online, you can go after them," says Molly Leahey, legislative counsel for the Newspaper Association of America (NAA), which has lobbied lawmakers to safeguard print and online newspaper products.

NAA has always argued "that copyright law applies to the Internet and that we didn't necessarily need" the new law, Leahey adds.

Newspapers hope the law will refute freewheeling Web site operators who argue they can reproduce published works in their entirety under "fair use" exceptions to copyright law.

---

2. Article by Tony Case from *Editor & Publisher* December 12, 1998. Copyright © *Editor & Publisher*. Reprinted with permission.

"There are a lot of myths out there about copyright law on the Internet," says Susan Crawford, partner of the Washington, D.C., law firm Wilmer Cutler & Pickering, which has represented the *Washington Post*, the *New York Times*, and online service providers and software companies. "Because there's so much information available, people assume, 'If it's up there, I can use it.' There's been an attempt to call this wholesale use 'fair use,' but that's not what the copyright law contemplates."

Meanwhile, fair-use provisions of the digital copyright act benefit newspapers in their own reporting role by protecting their ability to use material for news purposes, no matter where the information comes from, Leahey explains. The act calls for a two-year period to study how existing fair-use tenets work online.

Caroline Little, vice president and general counsel for the *Post*'s online unit, hopes the measure puts to rest any doubts that copyright protections extend to the digital domain. "There seems to be this feeling that the old copyright laws don't apply on the Internet," she says. The digital copyright law "clarifies what the ground rules are."

The *Post* and the *Los Angeles Times* recently filed suit against the producers of a California Web site, Free Republic, that posted articles from the two papers' online editions. Free Republic's attorney cited fair-use exceptions to copyright law. Little would not comment on the suit.

Rex Heinke, who represents the *Post* and *Los Angeles Times* for Los Angeles–based Gibson, Dunn & Crutcher, says the new law probably won't impact the case, since it is based on the theory of fair use.

Online Legislation Surges

It was a banner year for online legislation, as some 300 bills before Congress contained the word Internet, compared with 75 last year, the *New York Times* reported.

NAA president and CEO John F. Sturm expressed disappointment that Congress failed to pass a bill designed to protect electronic databases. The bill passed the House unanimously but was not taken up by the Senate. Sen. Orrin Hatch (R-Utah), the Judiciary Committee chairman, says he wants to move the legislation next session. NAA contends newspapers need the law to combat growing online piracy of classified ads.

Sturm says NAA wants "an additional but separate layer of protection for what we know to be compilation classifieds," and added safety for "databases in general."

Adds NAA counsel Leahey, "We believe the copyright law applies to databases. But in the event it doesn't, we want a second level of protection for our classified databases, which are an important revenue source for newspapers."

Washington attorney Crawford finds it curious that U.S. law, providing perhaps the strongest copyright protection in the world, has fallen behind on database protection and online piracy. . . .

The digital copyright law, while not a panacea for copyright security problems online, increases newspapers' sense of security that "their online versions are protected, just as their print versions are," says Barbara Wall, Gannett Co. vice president and senior legal counsel. While the law aids aggrieved publishers "somewhat," they need to remain vigilant about defending their intellectual property, since computer cut-and-paste functions make it so easy to lift material from Web sites.

Supreme Court Upholds Extended Copyrights[3]

The Associated Press, January 16, 2003

The Supreme Court sidestepped a confrontation with Congress over longer copyright protections for cartoon characters, songs, books and other creations worth billions of dollars.

Companies like The Walt Disney Co. were relieved at Wednesday's 7–2 court ruling, which upheld a 20-year copyright extension. Other groups and Internet publishers were disappointed that the court did not use the case to stop Congress from repeatedly extending copyrights.

Hundreds of thousands of books, movies and songs were close to being released into the public domain when Congress extended the copyright by 20 years in 1998 with a law named after the late Rep. Sonny Bono, R-Calif.

The Supreme Court said the law was neither unconstitutional overreaching by Congress, nor a violation of free-speech rights.

"The winners are folks who hold valuable copyrights. The losers are everyone else," said Erik S. Jaffe, a Washington attorney who filed arguments in the case. "Everyone is going to pay more for things they would have had for cheap or free."

New Hampshire Internet site publisher Eric Eldred, who challenged the extension, said the decision "seems like it's giving an open license to Congress to keep those works locked up perpetually."

Justice Ruth Bader Ginsburg wrote that the court was "not at liberty to second-guess congressional determinations and policy judgments of this order, however debatable or arguably unwise they may be."

But Justices John Paul Stevens and Stephen Breyer sharply disagreed.

"The serious public harm and the virtually nonexistent public benefit could not be more clear," Breyer wrote in his dissent.

Copyright holders stand to collect about $400 million more a year from older creations under the extension, he said. The limit on the use of information "threatens to interfere with efforts to preserve our nation's historical and cultural heritage" and to educate children, Breyer added.

---

3. Reprinted with permission of The Associated Press.

A contrary ruling would have caused huge losses for entertainment companies like Disney and AOL Time Warner Inc. AOL Time Warner had said an adverse ruling would threaten copyrights for such movies as *Casablanca*, *The Wizard of Oz* and *Gone With the Wind*.

Breyer said AOL Time Warner also owns the copyright of the song "Happy Birthday to You."

Also at risk of expiration was protection for the version of Mickey Mouse portrayed in Disney's earliest films, such as 1928's *Steamboat Willie*.

The ruling will affect movie studios and heirs of authors and composers. It will also affect small music publishers, orchestras and church choirs that must pay royalties to perform some pieces.

Disney spokeswoman Michelle Bergman said the decision "ensures copyright owners the proper incentive to originate creative works for the public to enjoy."

Members of Congress, as expected, were pleased.

"The copyright and related industries employ millions of American workers, and its vitality is critical to our national economy," House Judiciary Committee Chairman F. James Sensenbrenner, R-Wis., said.

Rep. John Conyers of Michigan, top Democrat on the House Judiciary Committee, said: "This decision demonstrates this country's commitment to encouraging authorship and free expression."

The Constitution allows Congress to give authors and inventors the exclusive right to their works for a "limited" time.

Congress has repeatedly lengthened the terms of copyrights. Copyrights lasted only 14 years in 1790. With the challenged 1998 extension, the period is now 70 years after the death of the creator. Works owned by corporations are now protected for 95 years.

The case is *Eldred vs. Ashcroft*, 01–618.

Broken Links and Broken Laws

Copyright Confusion Online[4]

BY JEFF BELLE
ECONTENT, FEBRUARY 2003

Don't blame Columba Kilmacolm. A religious man, and a lover of books, he borrowed a copy of St. Jerome's psalter from his old teacher Finnian and copied it himself word for word—by hand. His intention was to bring copies of St. Jerome to the masses. Finnian, a less charitable sort it seems, took exception to this and demanded Columba's copied manuscript be returned with the first copy. The resulting dispute came before the King, Dermott, who in a head-scratching bit of jurisprudence declared "as to every cow her calf, so to every book its offspring. Therefore, the copy of the psalter belongs to Finnian."

That was 6th-century Ireland, but the thinking behind copyright law has grown no less muddled since. Two major laws with implications for online copyright have been enacted within the last five years—the Sonny Bono Copyright Extension Act and the Digital Millennium Copyright Act (DMCA)—both of which include questionable provisions and cloudy expositions that may do more harm than good to content professionals.

Caught in a Mouse Trap

A millennium and a half after Dermott's perplexing pronouncement, Eric Eldred, another idealistic lover of books, began posting on his Web site digital versions of out-of-print literary texts by authors running the gamut from Guy de Maupassant to Mark Twain.

That Eldred could do this at all was part of the larger concern already raising eyebrows among intellectual property lawyers. Namely, that copyright laws could never be enforced within this new medium seemingly perfectly designed to thwart them. (Copy, paste, send. Rip, mix, burn.)

As a result, the death-knell for copyright sounded early on, but like Twain said, rumors of its death were greatly exaggerated. In fact just the opposite appeared to take place when Sonny Bono decided that copyright protection should be extended 20 additional years—to the outrage of Eldred, who filed suit—and the Clinton Administration enacted the DMCA.

---

4. Article by Jeff Belle from *EContent* February 2003. Copyright © *EContent*. Reprinted with permission.

This spring, the Supreme Court will issue a ruling on *Eldred vs. Ashcroft*, the high-water mark for those challenging the constitutionality of the Sonny Bono Extension. Eldred, the lead plaintiff, teamed up with lead lawyer, author (*Code, The Future of Ideas*) and Stanford professor Lawrence Lessig, who argued the case before the Court last October.

Eldred v. Ashcroft is, more than anything, about the tradeoff between private interests (read: large multinational media companies) and the public domain. The implications of this are obvious when you consider the flagship example of the countermovement that gave the act the nickname the Mickey Mouse Law. Namely, that *Steamboat Willie*, the first copyrighted work containing Mickey Mouse, was to revert, under the old law, into the public domain in 2003 (to be followed shortly by Donald Duck, Goofy, and the rest of the Disney gang).

The law now stipulates that copyright protection exists for the lifetime of the artist, plus 70 years—an extension of 20 years. The problem with all of this, in the plaintiffs' view, is that the framers of the Constitution never intended for this much protection. Furthermore, adding 20 years to copyright protection retroactively has no real impact on the future creators of content, but it has an enormous effect on someone whose rights are about to expire. Congress originally interpreted the Constitutional language (exclusive rights shall be granted to authors and inventors "for limited times") to calculate a copyright term of 28 years. Yet since 1964, Congress has extended the term of existing copyrights 11 times.

The *Eldred vs. Ashcroft* Web site explains the plaintiffs' position: "The biggest effect of these laws is to make unavailable an extraordinary range of creative material for next generation's creators. Just as Walt Disney used the works of the Brothers Grimm to produce some of the best of the Disney stories, so too should the next Walt Disney be able to build upon the stories told by Disney."

But "freeing the Mouse," as the plaintiffs' motto goes, is not the central tenet of the cause. More so, "this case is about freeing the vast majority of creative work still under copyright that no one seeks to protect," the plaintiffs say. "Congress sacrificed all these works, just to protect a few valuable copyrights."

Dilbert Gets Litigious

If Eric Eldred is the Columba to Disney's Finnian, Dan Wallach is a copyright law pioneer for another, much grayer issue surrounding online copyright issues. Around the time Eldred was uploading the public domain, Dan Wallach was breaking legal ground in a far subtler—and still emerging—question of copyright infringement in the age of hypertext linking.

Wallach, an avid fan of the Dilbert comic strips, found the layout of United Media's Official Dilbert Web site "really lame." And so, taking it upon himself to offer the world a better layout, he linked—the better to skirt the copyright issue—directly to United Media's Web server. He called his creation the Dilbert Hack Page.

"When you visited the Dilbert Hack Page, your browser would connect to United Media's server to download the images," Wallach explains. "However, it would present those images in a different fashion than United Media might have liked."

It didn't take long for UM's lawyers to come knocking. "Thank you for your enthusiasm," they wrote. "However, this material is copyrighted by United Feature Syndicate, Inc."

"I very carefully designed my Web page to avoid copyright problems," Wallach wrote back. "If you examine the HTML for my page, you will see it pulls images from the United Media server. I do not store any United Feature Syndicate intellectual property on my server. At the current time, copyright protection does not extend to URLs. Thus, I believe I am within my rights to present my Web page in its current form. Technically, I present a directory of pointers in much the same way as Yahoo!, Lycos, or AltaVista. The legality of my page is directly related to the legality of search engines in general, and any legal action against me would set an important precedent for intellectual property on the Web."

UM's reply: "If it turns out you are wrong, it will cost you a lot of money."

At that point, Wallach called a lawyer.

UM's chief complaint was that the Dilbert Hack Page did not link to the Dilbert site "in its entirety." "We offer our comics to readers free of charge," they said. "All we ask in return is the opportunity to sell advertising near these comics. By linking to just our comics, Mr. Wallach impairs our ability to generate revenues."

Wallach still explains his position this way: "Consider a VCR that can be programmed to grab every episode of a TV show and record them, sequentially, with commercials removed. The TV shows are

Illustration by Guy Junker

still broadcast on the air, but the VCR presents them in a fashion that is not how the original broadcasters intended. That's what the Dilbert Hack Page did."

"There's nothing to stop a viewer of the normal Dilbert pages from ignoring the advertising, whether by personal choice, or via software—such as WebWasher, my favorite—that automatically cuts out advertisements. Likewise, there's nothing to stop a VCR user from hitting the fast forward button. Even with live TV, you can always change channels during the commercials. Thus, it's hard to argue that the TV networks ever 'lose' any money when a viewer ignores the commercial. Advertisers already figure in that their 'hit rate' on such advertising is relatively low."

The issue was settled out of court and rather amicably (in no small part due to Wallach's sensibility in the matter), with Wallach agreeing to discontinue the Hack Page and UM agreeing to Wallach's documenting the dispute (which can be read for posterity at *www.cs.rice.edu/~dwallach/dilbert*).

But the issue of linking continues to confound. Hypertext linking is, after all, the fundamental architecture on which the World Wide Web is built. As such, attempts to control it through licensing are fraught with conflict.

You'd be forgiven for thinking that the 1998 passage of the Digital Millennium Copyright Act cleared some of these issues up. But because Wallach's dispute with UM came about prior to the 1998 enactment of DMCA—and there was no legal precedent at the time for the issues in dispute—it wasn't until the Ninth Circuit Court of Appeals in San Francisco ruled on a similar case last February that Wallach's intended defense was put to the test.

Under the aegis of DMCA, Leslie Kelly, a professional photographer, sued Arriba Soft Corp. (now Ditto.com), owner of a search engine that displays its results as thumbnail pictures rather than text. Double clicking on the thumbnails delivers a larger, in-lined image of the original image from its source location. Kelly claimed that Arriba's in-lining of his copyrighted work within its search results constituted infringement. The case's first hearing resulted in a ruling for Arriba; according to the court, Arriba's database of images constituted "fair use." Two years later, however, the appeals court both affirmed and reversed the lower court's opinion. "The creation and use of the thumbnails in the search engine is fair use," it said. "But the display of the larger image is a violation of Kelly's exclusive right to publicly display his works."

Instead of shedding light on the fundamental issue of intellectual property rights as they apply to hypertext linking, the *Kelly vs. Arriba* ruling—and by extension the DMCA—have only demonstrated the depth of the confusion over the matter.

Who Dunit?*

BY TYRA W. HILLIARD
SUCCESSFUL MEETINGS, MAY 2003

Whether or not you're consciously aware of it, meeting professionals deal with copyright issues on a daily basis. Tasks like recording conference presentations, printing meeting proceedings, or posting an article of interest on the organization's Web site all trigger concerns about copyright. Failure to understand who owns the copyright and how and when someone other than the copyright holder can use copyrighted material can result in copyright infringement.

Generally, the person who creates an original work—the "author"—is the holder of the copyright. An author's work is protected by copyright as soon as the work is "fixed in a tangible medium," whether or not a copyright notice is evident on the work and whether or not a copyright registration is filed with the U.S. Library of Congress. However, it is advisable to put a copyright notice on an original work to make others aware that the work is protected by copyright. A copyright notice contains a copyright designation, the year of first publication, and the name of the copyright holder. Example: © 2003, Tyra W. Hilliard, Esq.

However, there is a wide exception to this general rule for "works made for hire." In most cases, the copyright for works created by an employee belongs to the organization that the employee works for. That is, the organization "hires" the employee to, among other things, create these works on the organization's behalf.

The "work made for hire" doctrine may also apply when an organization contracts with another person or entity as an independent contractor to do work for the organization. For example, an organization may contract with an independent contractor to develop the organization's Web site content or translate conference proceedings into another language. To minimize the risk of a dispute arising over who "owns" the created work, the contract between the organization and the independent contractor should clearly spell out that the work is a "work made for hire" and that the copyright on the final product belongs to the organization.

Meeting planners must be certain to get permission from the owner of the copyright before reproducing an article, taping a presentation, or posting copyrighted material to a Web site. If written properly, an agreement between the planner's organization and the copyright holder can grant limited or extensive rights for reproduction or distribution of copyrighted works without threatening the copyright holder's legal rights. Such an agreement should clearly spell out who owns the copyright and what rights are granted to the other party.

Finding a Balance

If Eric Eldred and Dan Wallach have illustrated anything other than the confused state of current copyright law, it's that there is more money to be lost than made in the digital wilderness. At least that seems to be the position of Congress and the major media players who lobby it. Until the Internet is more opportunity than threat to the copyright holder, it will be difficult to strike a reasonable balance between private interests and the public domain.

But where should that balance be found? "The public has an interest in having public domain access to media conceived during its own lifetime," says Wallach. "If books, movies, and songs were not public domain until long after the deaths of the children to whom they were originally marketed, then those children never had any public domain benefit from those works. That seems to be a good litmus test for finding a balance."

There is more money to be lost than made in the digital wilderness.

In *The Future of Ideas*, Lawrence Lessig offers a similarly reasonable and explicit solution: "Work that an author publishes should be protected for a term of five years once registered, and that registration can be renewed fifteen times," Lessig declares. "If the registration is not renewed, then the work falls into the public domain."

To push ideas like these forward, Lessig and Eldred have teamed up again in a not-for-profit project called Creative Commons, an attempt to establish a set of more flexible intellectual property licenses that content creators can use—free of charge—to set their own rules for others' use of their work.

"Many people may prefer an alternative to this 'copyright by default,' particularly those who do their creating on the Internet," they say on their Web site. "Ironically, there is no easy way to announce that you intend to enforce only some of your rights, or none at all. At the same time—and again because copyright notice is optional—people who want to copy and reuse creative works have no reliable way to identify works available for such uses. We hope to provide some tools that solve both problems: a set of free public licenses sturdy enough to withstand a court's scrutiny, simple enough for non-lawyers to use, and yet sophisticated enough to be identified by various Web applications."

It's a worthy effort that deserves to succeed, and hopefully will go a long way toward filling in the holes in DMCA and delineating infringement from fair use. *Eldred vs. Ashcroft*, on the other hand, faces a tougher road. It's worth noting the Sonny Bono Extension originally passed the Senate without a single vote against it; Eldred and Lessig, alas, are being given little chance of victory. The Justices, while seemingly sympathetic to the cause, remain wary of their jurisdiction.

"It is hard to understand how, if the overall purpose of the Copyright Clause is to encourage creative work, how some retroactive extension could possibly do that. One wonders what was in the minds of the Congress," Justice Sandra Day O'Connor said in the argument phase. "But," she added, the question is, "is it unconstitutional?"

Columba Kilmacolm, not incidentally, was canonized St. Columba for his troubles, and is today the patron of bookbinders and poets. This spring, we'll see whether the Court is moved by his spirit—and applies the wisdom of King Solomon or the confusion of King Dermott to the Eldred case.

Copyright on the Web

What You Don't Know Can Cost You[5]

BY EMILY A. VANDER VEER
THE WRITER, MARCH 2001

"Congratulations!" gushed a friend. "I saw your latest article on XYZ.com, and it's terrific!" At the time, I'd never even visited XYZ.com, much less written for it—but a quick peek proved my friend wasn't mistaken. There, in living color, was the article I'd submitted just days before. The problem was, I'd submitted the piece to a different online publication.

As more and more writers are discovering, the benefits of the Internet—including an explosion of new paying markets, an inexpensive publicity channel and an efficient, convenient way to conduct research—come with a price. The very technology that makes the Web possible also makes it easy for publishers and individuals to reproduce and distribute a manuscript without the owner's permission. In other words, the Web dramatically increases the threat of copyright violation, whether you write for print, radio, television/film or online publications.

"I've discovered about 25 unauthorized [Web] reprints in the last year or so," says Amy Gahran, a freelance writer and editor. Like most professional writers who rely on reprints for income, Gahran takes the theft of her property seriously. "This is a business matter, pure and simple. No one ever did me a favor by stealing from me."

Copyright refers, quite literally, to the right to copy an executed work. In the United States, copyright conferral is automatic; the instant you complete a manuscript, you hold the copyright. (Formally registering your manuscript with the U.S. Copyright Office is an optional step that provides additional protection in the event of future litigation.)

But although the Internet doesn't alter the concept of copyright, it does affect the practical matter of tracking violations and enforcing copyrights online. The reason? Works can be obtained, reproduced and distributed via the Web with startling ease. "Sketching the Future of Copyright in a Networked World," a 1998 report commissioned by the U.S. Copyright Office, refers to this technological free-for-all as "decentralized infringement."

Here are two of the most common examples:

---

5. Article by Emily A. Vander Veer from *The Writer* March 2001. Copyright © Emily A. Vander Veer. Reprinted with permission.

- **The text of one of your pieces appears on a Web site you never heard of.** It takes just minutes to copy the text of an electronically published manuscript (or to scan a printed original) and display that pirated text on a Web site. Amateur Webmasters frequently ignore copyright notices in the mistaken belief that they're doing authors a favor by providing additional "exposure." However, copying a manuscript and reproducing it on a publicly viewable Web site without permission constitutes copyright violation, just as if the article were being reprinted in a traditional print magazine. (Note: Hyperlinks—underlined words that allow visitors to hop from one Web site to another when clicked—allow Web sites to link to the text of an article without actually copying it. Since no copying is involved, a hyperlink from a site to an article does not constitute copyright infringement.)
- **One or more of your previously published pieces appear in an archived database**. Increasingly, both online and print markets are demanding the right to archive material and make it available online, either for free or for a fee—often without offering additional compensation to the author. But in the absence of an explicit transfer of rights, no Web site has the authority to archive your work.

The question of whether electronic archives constitute separate, licensable rights was put to rest by *Tasini et al. vs. The New York Times et al.* In September 1999, a three-judge panel of the U.S. Court of Appeals ruled that *The New York Times* and other publishers cannot resell newspaper and magazine articles by means of electronic databases unless they have the freelance authors' express permission.

As the Web has grown, the incidence of copyright violation has increased; and so, predictably, has litigation. While Contentville.com sidestepped a lawsuit earlier this year by agreeing to work with the Publication Rights Clearinghouse (a collective licensing agency administered by the National Writers Union, or NWU), other lawsuits have been brought—including a class-action suit against UnCover, an Internet-based document delivery service.

While lawsuits and pressure from writers' organizations such as the NWU and the American Society of Journalists and Authors (ASJA) appear to be raising the visibility of electronic copyright issues, the wheels of justice are often slow to turn. For awhile, at least, it's up to writers to protect themselves from online theft.

Fortunately, there are several actions you can take to preserve your rights:

1. **Understand how copyright works.** If you don't have a working knowledge of copyright, spend a few minutes online to familiarize yourself with the way copyright works.

Copyright Primer

- Only executed works can be copyrighted. (A novel can be copyrighted; the idea for a novel cannot.)
- Copyright is automatic. A writer automatically owns the copyright to a work the second it is completed, even if the work isn't published. Caveat: If you intend to bring a lawsuit, you must first have registered your copyright with the U.S. Copyright Office or another governmental body if you live in another country. In addition, the timing of formal registration (within 90 days of the work's completion, vs. five or more years later) affects the damages you can claim in a lawsuit.
- Reproducing and publicly distributing a manuscript via the Web, e-mail or any other Internet protocol is considered "publishing" for the purpose of copyright.
- It's always best to have a signed contract in place when you sell your work, so that both parties understand precisely which rights are being granted.

Consider formally registering your work with the U.S. Copyright Office (or the office of your country). Doing so conveys rights that may be important if you're ever involved in a copyright-related lawsuit.

2. **Know what rights you're selling, and to whom.** Many writers begin work on a project only after they've reviewed and signed a written contract; without one, electronic rights are virtually impossible to enforce. In the print world, First North American Serial Rights (FNASR) are assumed in the absence of a contract stating otherwise—but since the Web is limited neither temporally nor geographically, FNASR don't apply. Without benefit of a contract, the rights you assume you're selling may not be the rights an electronic market assumes it's purchasing.

   "I sent a couple of sample pieces to the editorial director at a pre-launch dot-com because they were considering using me as an editor," says freelance writer Erica Manfred, who forwarded her work based on a verbal agreement rather than a written contract. "Next thing I know, I find one of my pieces up on their beta site under another name." Because the manuscript was electronically published in its entirety, it was vulnerable to theft by other publishers and individuals for the entire time it was displayed on that Web site. The company subsequently folded, and Manfred never heard back from the director.

3. **Log online clips.** If you contribute to electronic publications, get into the habit of using your browser to print a copy of each electronic clip the day it goes online. When you print a Web page, your browser adds the full Web address of the file and a date to the bottom of the printout, which you can then use to track publication details. This record could be useful during a

dispute—especially if the publishing Web site moves or archives your work.

4. **Search for your byline online.** Once a month or so, try typing your name into a few search engines and online directories. Doing so will display Web sites which have added your name—and possibly your work—directly to the text of their Web sites. Two to try: *MetaCrawler.com* (a "meta" search engine that searches several popular search engines at once) and *DejaNews.com* (a directory that searches all newsgroup posts). Also search for your name through online databases such as Lexis-Nexis, *www.lexis-nexis.com/lncc*. Unfortunately, many online databases require a registration fee.

   If you find an article that was posted online without your permission, print out a copy immediately, making sure to note the full Web address and the date.

5. **Attempt to negotiate.** Contact any editor, electronic list owner or e-mail poster who has reproduced your work without your permission, to negotiate payment and/or the removal of your manuscript.

   "In all cases but one, I have been able to get my work removed, and in most cases have been able to get payment," says Gahran, who emphasizes that success sometimes requires persistence. "It helps to set a deadline and say, 'If I don't receive my full restitution fee by this date, I will publicize your theft.'"

6. **Take it to the next level.** If contacting the copyright violator directly doesn't work, contact the Internet service provider or Webmaster responsible for hosting the offending site and explain the situation. Most ISPs will shut down a site that's engaging in suspicious practices if you have documentation to prove it.

7. **Turn it over to the pros.** If all else fails, contact a writers' organization or legal counsel. "I joined the NWU," says Caron Golden, a freelancer who discovered that more than 50 articles she originally wrote for *The San Diego Union-Tribune*—and to which she retained full reprint rights—had been included in online databases without her permission. "They [the NWU] are working with me and about 30 other writers to resolve the issue."

8. **Stay in the loop.** Online writing communities are often the first to hear about copyright issues such as out-of-court settlements and class-action lawsuits.

9. **Investigate licensing agencies.** The NWU, ASJA and other organizations have set up digital licensing and reprint services to track online reprints, collect fees from publishers and forward those fees on to the rightful copyright owners—much like the music industry fixtures ASCAP (the American Society of Composers, Authors and Publishers) and BMI (Broadcast Music

Inc.). While the long-term success of these agencies depends in large part on the participation of publishers, they offer writers an alternative, low-cost way to help preserve copyrights online.

The software and publishing industries recently combined forces to develop a standard, widely implemented document delivery format that's both easy to distribute and impervious to online theft. But until it's successful, it's up to you to protect your own rights in cyberspace.

Poetic License

What Every Poet Should Know About Copyright[6]

BY TONYA MARIE EVANS
BLACK ISSUES BOOK REVIEW, JULY/AUGUST 2002

No one word is more misused or misunderstood within the written-and spoken-word communities than the term "copyright."

For writers, this single word creates more confusion and lends itself to more misinterpretation than the most perplexing verse ever penned. So I begin this article with a simple definition of this mystifying term. In the case of literary works, "copyright" is the exclusive right to make copies of the work, to make derivative works from the original (i.e., develop a stage play based on a poem), to distribute copies, to perform the work publicly and to authorize or prevent others from doing any or all of the above.

It is also important to distinguish copyright from other forms of intellectual property. A copyright protects an original artistic or literary work (e.g., a poem or poetry book), a patent protects an invention (e.g., the Palm Pilot), and a trademark (associated with goods) or service mark (associated with a service) protects a word, phrase, symbol or device (collectively referred to as a "mark") used in commerce to identify and distinguish one product or service from another, for example—Def Poetry Jam.

Unfortunately, some writers mistakenly believe that their copyright does not exist until they send their work to the Library of Congress. Worse yet, some are still under the erroneous impression that their work is "protected" because they send it to themselves in the mail! If you learn nothing else, understand this: the mail-yourself-the-poem-and-then-you'll-be-protected belief is a myth. It is simply not true, and hopefully no one reading this article will perpetuate this myth. Rest assured, the only thing you will prove when you mail your work to yourself is that the post office is still in the business of delivering mail.

The "mail myth" evolved in the days before the 1989 amendment to the Copyright Act, when the United States joined the Berne Convention. Under prior copyright law, authors were required to include a copyright symbol on their work in order to protect their work. Many rights were lost under the old law because of the strict copyright symbol requirement, as well as other formalities. Writers

---

6. Article by attorney Tonya Marie Evans, author of *Literary Law Guide for Authors* (2003/LE Series Books), from *Black Issues Book Review* (July–August 2002). Copyright 2002 © Tonya Marie Evans. Reprinted with permission.

believed that the only way to prove the existence of that work on a particular date was to mail a copy to themselves. However, this was neither necessary nor helpful.

So, you ask, how is a copyright created? Copyright is secured automatically upon creation once your work is fixed in a "tangible form." For instance, at the moment you write or record your poetry, your copyright in that work is secured. Note, however, that if you do a live performance of your work "freestyle," or from memory without first reducing it to writing or recording it, no copyright exists in that freestyle performance at that time. Nonetheless, simultaneous recording can create copyright; for instance, in the case of radio broadcasts, taped live performances and live televised sporting events.

So, you ask, if the copyright exists automatically, why register my copyright? Good question. Now I've got you thinking. Read on.

One good reason to register is to establish a public record of your copyright. Another compelling reason is the requirement that you register your work before you can file a lawsuit. You may also be able to avail yourself of other valuable rights if you win, like attorney fees and statutory damages.

My life's mission is to educate wordsmiths about the nature of copyright so that writers will be better equipped to secure and protect their creations and use the law to their advantage.

How Long Does Copyright Registration Take?

A copyright registration is effective on the date of receipt in the Copyright Office of all required elements in acceptable form, regardless of the length of time it takes to process the application and mail the certificate of registration. The length of time required by the Copyright Office to process an application varies from time to time, depending on the amount of material received. Remember that it takes a number of days for mail to reach the Copyright Office and for the certificate of registration to reach the recipient after being mailed from the Copyright Office.

You will receive no acknowledgment that your application for copyright registration has been received (the Office receives more than 500,000 applications annually), but you may expect:

- A letter or telephone call from a Copyright Office staff member if further information is needed; and
- A certificate of registration to indicate the work has been registered, or if the application cannot be accepted, a letter explaining why it has been rejected.

You might not receive either of these until approximately 8 months after submission.

If you want to know when the Copyright Office received your material, send it via registered or certified mail and request a return receipt.

For further information, write:

Library of Congress
Copyright Office
Information Section, LM-401
101 Independence Ave., S.E.
Washington, D.C. 20559-6000

If you need additional application forms for copyright registration, call (202) 707-9100 at any time. Leave your request as a recorded message on the Copyright Office Forms and Publications Hotline in Washington, D.C. Please specify the kind and number of forms you need. If you have general information questions and wish to talk to an information specialist, call (202) 707-3000, TTY (202) 707-6737.

You may also photocopy blank application forms; **however**, photocopied forms submitted to the Copyright Office must be clear, legible, on a good grade of 8½-inch by 11-inch white paper suitable for automatic feeding through a scanner/photocopier. The forms should be printed, preferably in black ink, head-to-head (so that when you turn the sheet over, the top of page 2 is directly behind the top of page 1). **Forms not meeting these requirements will be returned to the originator**.

All U.S. Copyright Office application forms are available from the Copyright Office Web site at ***www.loc.gov/copyright***. They may be downloaded and printed for use in registering a claim to copyright or for use in renewing a claim to copyright.

You must have Adobe Acrobat Reader installed on your computer to view and print the forms. The free Adobe® Acrobat® Reader may be downloaded from Adobe Systems Incorporated through links from the same Internet site at which the forms are available.

Print forms head-to-head (top of page 2 is directly behind the top of page 1) on a single piece of good-quality, 8½-inch by 11-inch white paper. To achieve the best-quality copies of the application forms, use a laser printer.

Frequently requested Copyright Office circulars, announcements, and recently proposed as well as final regulations are also available from the Copyright Office Web site.

Copyright Office circulars and announcements are available via fax. Call **(202) 707-2600** from any touchtone telephone. Key in your fax number at the prompt and the document number of the item(s) you want to receive by fax. The item(s) will be transmitted to your fax machine. If you do not know the document number of the item(s) you want, you may request that a menu be faxed to you. You may order up to three items at a time. Note that copyright application forms are *not* available by fax.

Source: Library of Congress, Copyright Office, 1999.

Who Owns History?[7]

BY JASON WILLIAMS
EDITOR & PUBLISHER, DECEMBER 11, 1999

When Jonathan Tasini, president of the National Writers Union, emerged victorious from the U.S. Court of Appeals in late September, he spoke as if he had slung a stone for struggling free-lancers everywhere and brought down a few giants of the media world—the New York Times Co. Inc., Newsday Inc., and the Time Inc. Magazine Co. Among his other targets: two monolithic database companies—Mead Data Central Corp. (parent of Lexis-Nexis) and University Microfilms International.

But the decision may have opened a Pandora's box that could seriously disrupt the continuity of the historical record that newspaper and magazine articles provide.

The court found that the New York Times Co. and the other defendants were infringing on the copyrights of the plaintiffs—a group of seven free-lancers led by Tasini—by including them in their electronic databases without the writers' express permission.

The ruling, a reversal of an earlier U.S. District Court decision, may well become a landmark media-law case because it could lead to the wholesale excising of an enormous number of articles from electronic archives and, possibly, huge financial losses for the newspaper and magazine industries.

In a post-victory press statement, Tasini sounded like Gen. George S. Patton rallying his troops for the final assault.

"Thanks to their own greed and arrogance, the media industry faces the grim reality of a tidal wave of lawsuits that will boggle their minds. . . . And let me be clear: Writers are prepared to go down the path of war," Tasini said, the rattle of his saber loud and clear.

Tasini guesses the number of free-lance articles archived in violation of copyright law to be in the tens of thousands. "There's no question that they face a huge liability for [infringements] of the past," he says.

Defense attorney Peter Johnson of the New York firm Debevoise & Plimpton believes the decision will be extremely detrimental to the media industry. If the decision stands, content as far back as 1976 could be removed en masse from the databases, leaving huge gaps and badly damaging research capabilities, he says.

---

7. Article by Jason Williams from *Editor & Publisher* December 11, 1999. Copyright © *Editor & Publisher*. Reprinted with permission.

From "Op-Ed pieces by politicians" to "high-school football student stringers," publishers could decide to remove all questionable content to avoid potential lawsuits, he says.

Most present free-lance contracts, however, have been carefully worded to include the transfer of "all rights" to the publisher and would not be affected by the ruling.

The Legal Issues

The point of contention in the case was Section 201(c) of the Copyright Act of 1976, which deals with contributions to "collective works." That is, any periodical issue, anthology, or encyclopedia where individual works are constructed to form a whole. Section 201(c) allows a publisher "the privilege of reproducing and distributing the contribution as part of that particular collective work, any revision of that collective work, and any later collective work in the same series," upon submittal of an article for publishing.

The U.S. District Court for the Southern District of New York deemed electronic database articles as "revisions of that collective work" and therefore exempted the databases from copyright infringement as valid "revisions" of the original publications, but the U.S. Court of Appeals reversed the decision Sept. 24.

> ***"The worst part . . . is the concept that a newspaper loses its identity when it is placed online."*****—Bruce Keller, lawyer**

A three-judge panel ruled that "the most natural reading of 'revision' of 'that collective work' clause" is that it "protects only later editions of a particular issue of a periodical, such as the final [evening] edition of a newspaper." The court criticized the previous ruling for defining "revision of that collective work" too broadly and allowing the exemption "to swallow the rule."

Bruce Keller, another defense attorney associated with Debevoise & Plimpton, says he believes the appellate court misapplied the term "collective work" to electronic databases, which he says are more accurately labeled as "electronic libraries."

"The worst part of this decision is the concept that a newspaper loses its identity when it is placed online," says Keller.

Johnson says he believes the court "failed to look at the legislative history of the revision clause." He contends that the court's interpretation of a "revision of that collective work" is too narrow in its insistence that the arrangement of individual works must be retained.

Since the landmark decision was handed down, Tasini's vigor hasn't dimmed, despite an Oct. 8 petition filed by the defendants asking for a review of the three-judge decision by the whole court, a rehearing en banc, in legalese.

"It's a delay tactic," says Tasini, who is confident that the ruling, authored by Chief Judge Ralph K. Winter, will be upheld and that the industry will finally have to address the "continuous" infringement caused by their databases.

Keller balks at the idea that the review request is a delaying tactic. "It is a procedural process taken when one thinks the decision is wrong," says Keller.

But what is evident in the wording of the petition is that newspaper companies are genuinely concerned about the consequences of the decision, not just to themselves but to the industry.

"[T]he Panel Opinion suddenly exposes all publishers of newspapers, magazines, anthologies, and other collective works to enormous potential liability for having preserved the contents of their publications on microfilm, [on] CD-ROM, and in electronic libraries such as Nexis," reads the brief.

It is the first time they have admitted on record that they are at financial risk, says Tasini, and he's more than willing to press the point with newspaper investors. Tasini has sent letters to several large pension funds warning them of the "enormous potential liability" threatening their investments.

"It is safe to assume," reads the letter, "that virtually all media companies (print publishers, electronic databases, and other information aggregators) are potentially using copyrighted works illegally. . . . Liabilities for individual companies will vary depending on the amount of free-lance material used."

Keller, however, is quick to assert that the "potential liability" would result in newspapers being forced to remove a plethora of articles from their electronic databases.

"This is not a case of money damages," says Keller. The Tasini case is not a class-action suit, so therefore damages awarded—if appeals are denied—would be only to the seven plaintiffs in the case and would be "as low as $250" for Tasini himself, says Keller.

Because it is a case of "innocent infringement," he says, Tasini and the other plaintiffs would have to prove that someone had actually read his article online and then prove that the publishers had profited from it, which will be extremely difficult. "The [Lexis-Nexis] system was designed at a time when it was not possible to track per article," says Keller.

A Giant Undertaking

When asked, most newspaper and database companies will not or cannot provide an exact number of free-lance articles archived. Two database companies, Lexis-Nexis, which is a defendant in the case, and Infonautics, which is not, do not track the work status of document authors, according to company officials.

"The customary practice in the information industry is for the publisher to be responsible for obtaining all necessary copyright interests for online distribution," reads a prepared statement by

Lexis-Nexis. Lexis-Nexis' database contains 2.5 billion searchable documents and about 1,000 newspapers from which articles are obtained and archived.

Infonautics, a smaller database company with more than 7 million documents, two-thirds of which are newspaper articles, takes a similar stance, deferring to its clients' wishes.

"If the publisher tells us to take [certain free-lance articles] off, we would have to take it off," says Bill Burger, vice president of content at Infonautics. "No one knows what effect [the decision] will have."

Future Transactions

Current free-lance usage varies widely from publication to publication. At the *Washington Post*, where free-lancing is handled on a departmental basis, the national desk reports that it uses three or four free-lancers regularly, while the style desk uses about 20.

According to Assistant Managing Editor Shirley Carswell, free-lance contracts have included electronic right for two to three years, which suggests that its databases may be infringing the copyrights of free-lancers used before 1996.

On the other end of the spectrum, the tiny *Daily Challenge*, an African-American-oriented, 79,540-circulation paper in New York, continues business as usual. Editor Dawad Philip estimates that about 30 percent of his editorial content is by free-lancers, but he requires no formal contract, confident that his free-lancers are happy with the arrangements made.

The Cox-owned *Atlanta Journal and Constitution* deals with free-lancers like most newspapers today. Their free-lance contracts specifically state that "Cox Newspapers will have first right to publish the work in our printed newspapers. While the contributor retains original copyright and ownership, we will retain the right to the published work for inclusion in other Cox Newspapers compilations. Our rights specifically include the rights to distribute the work through our Internet services [and] in our electronic databases, and to republish it as part of any reprint, electronic or otherwise."

The language of the contract is careful to include all Cox newspapers as well as electronic publishing. According to Tasini, newspaper companies cannot limit the wording to databases as all electronic mediums could be in danger of copyright infringement once the information is digitized, in any form.

"The decision could be applied to any secondary uses in the digital world," says Tasini, which means newspaper Web sites also could be violating the copyright law by posting, without permission, free-lance stories that appeared in the print versions.

Past Transactions

But even if a particular newspaper company has been securing electronic copyrights for several years, the potential for liability stretches back to 1976, when the copyright act was passed, because no newspapers have been regularly securing electronic rights for that long.

"[The Tasini decision] probably won't mean that much to the industry, going forward," says new-media attorney Eric Bergner of the New York–based Moses & Singer law firm, except that the contracts will be more carefully worded to secure online rights.

Going back, however, Bergner predicts that the decision to remove potential infringing articles will be an easy one for newspapers that examine the costs and benefits of paying for the electronic rights vs. removing the stories from the databases.

"It's a monumental task," Bergner says, referring to the arduous process of tracking down the offending articles and then the authors themselves to purchase retroactive licenses.

The fact that a media company would rather drop articles than pay for them "shows the low moral standard under which these companies are operating."—
Jonathan Tasini, president National Writers Union

"Is it worth it for [newspaper companies] to go through and determine who was a free-lancer and who was work-for-hire?" asks Bergner. In addition, writers could conceivably argue under the Tasini precedent that every time a new article is added to the database it becomes a new "collective work" and hence a new infringement each time.

"It could potentially destroy all electronic research ability," Bergner says, echoing Johnson's sentiments, because publishers would remove the content to avoid liability.

The fact that a media company would rather drop articles than pay for them "shows the low moral standard under which these companies are operating," says Tasini.

Free-lancers, not surprisingly, agree. "[The removal of infringing articles] strikes me as an obnoxious view of the importance of journalism, but, then, I would expect it," says New York free-lancer Dylan Foley, who has written for the *Boston Globe* and the *Globe and Mail* in Toronto.

Valerie Sweeten, a Houston-based free-lancer who has written for the *Houston Chronicle* and *People* magazine, agrees that publishers should pay for any additional publishing, although it was the first she had heard of the decision.

Todd Carter, a free-lancer from Jenison, Mich., and a member of NWU, believes the decision is a positive step towards accountability. "You shouldn't sign your rights away," he says, but he admits it is difficult for less-experienced free-lancers to negotiate a favorable contract.

Keller bristles at the idea that removal of the articles is indicative of a "low moral standard," calling Tasini's demands for additional payments to free-lancers "outrageous" and "unrealistic."

A "Simple Solution"

Tasini claims he has a "simple solution" to the enormous undertaking that settling accounts would take—in the Publication Rights Clearinghouse (PRC). The PRC offers retroactive copyright licenses to publishers for the free-lance works of its enrollees.

Then, 75 percent to 90 percent of the licensing fee goes to PRC writers, according to the NWU Web site. In essence, the PRC acts as the "middle man" between the publishers and the free-lancers. The fee for free-lancers to sign up for the PRC is $20 for NWU members and $40 for nonmembers.

According to a press release issued by Tasini, the PRC has already brought more than $13,000 to 92 union members, with one member receiving $1,719.

The PRC is partnered with the Copyright Clearance Center (CCC), "the largest licensor of photocopy reproduction rights in the world," reads the release. The CCC handles all processing of the licensing requests.

"It is inherently unfair: The publishers already paid for these articles," says Keller. "This idea of a Publication Rights Clearinghouse is going nowhere. I have yet to hear of a single publisher interested in a clearinghouse."

Although Tasini refuses to comment on any future legal action, the next step for the NWU could be a class-action lawsuit, which would hold the whole industry accountable for electronic-rights infringements.

When the possibility of a class-action suit is raised, Johnson says, "I couldn't tell you how we would deal with that. One option would be to reduce the liability by wholesale excising of the database." But the defense isn't ready to call it quits on the current litigation, determined to take it to the U.S. Supreme Court if necessary.

In its official response to the case, Lexis-Nexis warned of the damages the decision could ultimately cause: "[T]he only complete historical record of what print media covered that one can be assured of will be hard-copy back issues of newspapers and magazines."

IV. 21st-Century Piracy

Editor's Introduction

Piracy has changed significantly since the days when Captain Kidd and Blackbeard terrorized ships on the high seas. If one were asked a few years ago what came to mind when the word "piracy" was mentioned, one would probably say men in eye patches and tattered clothing on ships looking to overrun commercial vessels for riches. Today, however, the word "piracy" has taken on a whole new meaning. In the high-tech digital age, a pirate can be anyone from a 10-year-old honor student to a 70-year-old grandmother. Today's robberies are more prevalent on the information superhighway than on the Caribbean. Yesterday's pirate ships are replaced by today's Web-accessible computers, and riches are no longer gold and gems but copies of songs, books, TV shows, and movies. These days piracy is harder to detect and to punish—but the entertainment industry is looking to change all that. What defines piracy in the 21st century? According to Dictionary.com, although the word "piracy" still refers to a "robbery at sea," it has also broadened its definition to mean "the unauthorized use or reproduction of copyrighted or patented material: *software piracy*." It is the latter definition that concerns Chapter 4, "21st-Century Piracy."

The first article in this section, "The New Napsters," discusses the service that made software piracy infamous—Napster—and the aftermath of its termination. Once Napster was shut down, other Napster-like services, such as Kazaa, Morpheus, and Grokster, started to fill the void that Napster had left in its wake. This article addresses the differences between Napster and these new services, as well as why the new services are harder to shut down and therefore may be here to stay.

With so many new Web sites appearing offering free music, the music industry needed to find a way to reclaim its territory while still generating revenue. The solution: pay-for-play Web sites. Matt Richtel looks at this new wave in music consumption in "Dollars 4 Downloads." Richtel examines specific sites and how much their services cost, as well as how many downloads a month customers receive, whether or not the sites allow CD burns, and if and when the services expire, requiring customers to pay again.

"It's All Free" looks at piracy through the eyes of the entertainment industry. Though the article deals mainly with the music industry and how it is being affected by illegal downloading, it also emphasizes how the TV and film industries are concerned with the future of their outlets based on what they have seen happen in the music business. This article not only describes how music labels such as EMI are trying to remedy the situation internally, but also how the entertainment industry is now turning to the law and suing individuals instead of merely trying to shut down online services. It also discusses online for-pay services which legally allow users to download music, movies, and TV shows for a fee, and the growing phenomenon of international piracy.

Those in the music industry have recently sought an alternate method to protect themselves from the piracy of their products. In his article "A New Tactic in the Download War," David Segal explains this new technique, called "spoofing." Spoofing, according to Segal, provides "repetitive loops or snippets filled with crackle and hiss" which people download believing the files are of high quality. These sabotaged versions prevent digital pirates from gaining legitimate versions of songs, and thus cut down on genuine versions floating around freely in cyberspace.

Spoofing may help protect the music industry, but other media outlets need to safeguard their intellectual property as well. "Make Copyright Law User-Friendly" discusses what needs to be done to protect software. Paul Brennan examines attempts at establishing consistency in laws among nations within the European Union, technical measures that can be taken to prevent fraud, and the need for an updated system of punishment for violators. Brennan also stresses the importance of establishing better software protections and the need for everyone to work together to protect the industry at large.

Although piracy has become an international epidemic, sometimes the culprits are right next door. "Gauging TV's 'Net Effect," by Paige Albiniak, looks at Canadian-based iCraveTV.com and the uproar it has caused, not only in the U.S., but in Canada as well. iCraveTV.com is a small Internet company that was illegally showing Canadian and U.S. television programs over the Internet. Albiniak explains that, even though the TV industry has not been hit as hard as the music industry, networks still have reason to worry that the music industry's present struggles are a foreshadowing of TV's future circumstances.

While the TV industry is fighting illegal piracy online, a legal form is sweeping the nation. The culprit is TiVo, a recording device that allows viewers to record programs and watch them later, usually omitting commercials. "Powell Preaching the Wonders of TiVo," by David Bloom and Pamela McClintock, looks at the TiVo revolution and its current and potential impact on commercial television.

The movie industry's own struggle against piracy is the subject of the chapter's final article, which considers a new and unusual threat. The operators of a chain of video stores in Colorado called Clean Flicks have been editing out what they deem inappropriate scenes, language, and other material from many of the movies they offer in order to make them more family-oriented and appropriate for younger or more conservative viewers. The problem, however, is that the directors of the altered videos feel that the editing violates the integrity of their films and detracts from the director's vision. Because the directors, such as Steven Spielberg and Martin Scorsese, involved in the case *Clean Flicks v. Hollywood* do not hold the copyrights to the films, their fight is a little more difficult than it might be otherwise. "*Clean Flicks v. Hollywood*: Intellectual Property Owners Losing Control," by Scott W. Breedlove, discusses this court case, the facts surrounding it, and other laws and previous court cases that could play a role in the decision.

The New Napsters[1]

BY MELANIE WARNER
FORTUNE, AUGUST 12, 2002

To the big record labels, Napster wasn't just a nuisance; it was their worst nightmare—the online equivalent to everyone storming into record stores and making off with armfuls of CDs. So when an appeals court issued an order last July forcing Napster to shut down, there was a sigh of relief throughout the recording industry. It was the day free music died.

Or so it seemed. Napster as we knew it is gone. But what's taken its place is a lot scarier for the music industry—and perhaps unstoppable. They're called file-sharing services, or P2P networks in geek-speak, and the three most popular ones—Kazaa, Grokster, and Morpheus—have a combined 70 million active users, compared with only 20 million for Napster in its heyday. Oh, and it's not just music being zapped across the Internet anymore. The new Napsters house video games, software programs, and movies, including ones now playing in theaters.

Not surprisingly, the big labels and the movie industry are trying to do to Kazaa, Grokster, and Morpheus what they did to Napster—litigate them out of existence. Only this time the outlaw networks may not be so easy to shut down. Kazaa, Grokster, and Morpheus work much the same way Napster did, but they're technologically smarter and, in a legal sense, a lot more amorphous. The Recording Industry Association of America (RIAA), representing eight record labels, and the Motion Picture Association, working on behalf of 19 movie studios, are suing the companies that own Kazaa, Grokster, and Morpheus—Sharman Networks, Grokster, and StreamCast Networks, respectively. (All three deny the charges.) But those entities don't run their networks the way, say, Sony does its record label; they have little control over what they created and can't tell who's downloading what file, whether it's an Eminem song or Grandma's recipe for blueberry pie. Thus the legal question becomes: If you can't control or see illegal activity, how can you be liable for it? In a memo leaked last December, the RIAA's legal team acknowledged that its claims against Kazaa, Grokster, and Morpheus "are not as strong as those against Napster."

What's more, even if there were a court order to shut down the networks, it may be impossible to do so. Napster operated with central servers that tracked and controlled the transfer of files

1. Article from *Fortune* August 12, 2002.

between users, but Kazaa, Grokster, and Morpheus are completely decentralized. Niklas Zennstrom, one of the two creators of Kazaa, says that the only way the system can be shut down is if every user elected to disable his program. That, of course, isn't very likely to happen.

The beauty (or menace, depending on which side you're on) of the P2P networks is that they've taken on a life of their own. No one understands that better than Zennstrom, 36, and his 26-year-old partner, Janus Friis. Working out of a small office in Amsterdam, they put Kazaa on the Web in the fall of 2000 as an experiment, expecting maybe a few thousand people would download it. But after the ninth circuit appeals court dealt Napster its first crushing blow in February 2001, millions of Napster users flocked to the site.

The stampede scared even Zennstrom and Friis. They began frantically searching for someone to buy Kazaa, ultimately finding a British-born woman in Australia named Nikki Hemming, who quickly rounded up a couple of investors and formed Sharman. Zennstrom and Friis are still on the hook legally because they kept the underlying software, called FastTrack, that powers Kazaa and Grokster. The RIAA and MPA recently added both men to the lawsuit as individuals.

The beauty . . . of the P2P networks is that they've taken on a life of their own.

Like Kazaa, Grokster and Morpheus also grew by themselves. None of the networks has ever done a stitch of marketing to lure users. Digital-music fans go wherever there's software that lets them get their MP3 files. Short of suing 70 million-plus people or encrypting every CD and DVD sold (an unlikely scenario), it's hard to imagine how to stop it.

Still, the music industry has to try. Global sales of CDs have been falling; last year they were down 5 percent, and for the first time blank CD sales outnumbered sales for recorded CDs. "You really have no choice," says Cary Sherman, the RIAA's general counsel. "If you don't bring lawsuits, then thousands more of these networks will develop rather than the handful that pop up periodically."

Part of the RIAA's legal strategy is to show that Kazaa, Grokster, and Morpheus are guilty because they knowingly chose to design software that prevented them from having any control. "StreamCast was originally a centralized system, and after the Napster decision they became a licensee of FastTrack because they thought they could evade the court's judgment," argues Sherman. The RIAA also hopes to make an issue out of the fact that both Sharman and Grokster are incorporated offshore, the former in Vanuatu, a group of islands in the South Pacific, and the latter in Nevis, a 36-square-mile tourist paradise in the West Indies. (Morpheus is based in Franklin, Tenn.) "When Kazaa was about to get an injunction by a court in the Netherlands, it sold its assets to a company in Australia, and then they incorporated in Vanuatu, where there is no copyright law," steams Sherman. Hemming, speaking recently from her office in Sydney, says that the Vanuatu move was for tax purposes only, and that Sharman, whose headquarters are in Australia, intends to follow Australian law.

The RIAA is considering a far riskier strategy—suing individuals who share large numbers of files on Kazaa, Grokster, or Morpheus. It's a tactic guaranteed to infuriate and alienate music fans, and it underscores the awful bind record labels are in. "This is a time of crisis for the music industry, and the RIAA is trying to fight a battle on multiple fronts," says Susan Kevorkian, an analyst at IDC.

Unfortunately, the industry isn't putting up much of a fight on perhaps the most important front: creating Internet services that people actually like for legitimately licensed music. The RIAA can file lawsuits until it's blue in the face, but unless there are attractive legal alternatives, people will probably continue flocking to what record executives call the "pirates." P.J. McNealy, an analyst

Unless there are attractive legal alternatives, people will probably continue flocking to what record executives call the "pirates."

at GartnerG2, estimates that at least 15 percent of the people using P2P networks would be willing to at least consider paying for their music if it were packaged in an appealing way.

But it's not. Late last year several big record labels launched three online music subscription services, none of which is exactly the Amazon.com of online music. Pressplay and MusicNet have crippling restrictions on how much music you can download or burn onto a CD each month, and the songs that you do download basically self-destruct once you stop being a customer. EMusic, which is owned by Vivendi Universal, lets you own the music, but it uses the nonrestrictive MP3 format, and thus none of the major music labels want to deal with it, including, ironically, Vivendi's own Universal Music Group. The result is a narrow selection of obscure music from small, independent labels—more Nusrat Fateh Ali Khan than Moby.

Alan McGlade, CEO of MusicNet, which is owned jointly by Sony Music and Universal Music, says that improving MusicNet's offerings is a top priority. But he admits that it's a slow, painstaking ordeal. "This is an industry in formation, and there's no infrastructure," he says. "It's not necessarily clear within any label who's responsible for servicing content to us or how it's going to be licensed."

Meanwhile, hundreds of thousands of new users join the P2P party every week. Today it's Kazaa, Morpheus, and Grokster, plus four or five others. And if those networks somehow get shut down, others will pop up in their place. "These networks are just tools to get what I want," a Kazaa user named ErikZ said in an e-mail. "If the record industry breaks these tools, you go out and find another."

Dollars 4 Downloads[2]

BY MATT RICHTEL
THE NEW YORK TIMES UPFRONT, JANUARY 21, 2002

Music's move from record stores to the Internet is raising plenty of questions, among them: Are the people who run the major record companies brain dead? Harsh, perhaps, but even record executives have been asking it of themselves.

The question is central to the online music debate. The five biggest record companies control about 85 percent of the music sold in the U.S. Last July, they sued and virtually shut down the Internet's most popular music-swapping service, Napster, and went after other sites that distribute copyrighted music without paying for it. Then, to fill the digital-music vacuum when listeners were clamoring for online alternatives, the record labels gave them . . . nothing.

Some fear the companies may have blown their chance to capture millions of fans. Since the summer, users have flocked to emerging online services like FastTrack, which has become more popular than Napster ever was. Only now are the labels finally getting their acts together with official, pay-for-play sites. They're deciding how users can buy music online, how much it will cost, and what users will be able to do with it. Is that better than nothing? Maybe not.

Searching for Songs

One point is beyond dispute: There is a growing demand for music online, especially among teens, as traditional CD sales are slipping. A survey by the Pew Internet and American Life Project last year found that 53 percent of online teens download music. Among 15- to 17-year-old boys online, the figure was 73 percent. More than 80 million people had downloaded Napster's software before last July.

To take Napster's place, the five top record companies decided to launch two subscription services. AOL Time Warner, Bertelsmann, and EMI backed MusicNet, with a stable of artists including the Dave Matthews Band, Kid Rock, and Faith Hill. Universal and Sony—who have Destiny's Child, Shakira, and many more—financed Pressplay. The services were originally scheduled to launch last summer, then late summer, then in the fall. MusicNet and Pressplay didn't actually debut until last month.

---

2. From *The New York Times Upfront* magazine, January 21, 2002 issue.

In the meantime, Napster's top successor became the FastTrack network, which allows users to freely exchange music online, download and listen to it on their computers, move it to portable MP3 players, and even burn their own CDs. FastTrack tries to get around Napster's copyright problems by leaving the music swapping only between users, peer to peer, without involving its own computers, as Napster did. FastTrack offers free file-swapping software called Morpheus, KaZaA, and Grokster; if people use that to swap copyrighted music, FastTrack sees no evil and hears no evil.

***"We have to make buying music as easy as stealing it."*—Jay Samit, Senior VP at EMI**

The major record labels sued the FastTrack sites and others in October, even while their own services were still no-shows. "Lawsuits are meaningless unless they are coupled with a strategy for providing a legitimate service," says Eric Scheirer, an analyst who follows the music industry for Forrester Research. For months, the record companies made "no real progress" in putting music online, he says.

Behind the Music Holdup

Critics say the labels dragged their feet, perhaps to preserve CD sales. But company executives say they were grappling with the business, legal, and technical complications of moving an entire industry from the physical world to cyberspace. They had to get permission from musicians to distribute their recordings online. They had to protect songs with encryption so that music could not be freely exchanged over the Internet. And they had to figure out a way to have users pay for it.

Jay Samit, senior vice president for new media with the EMI label, has followed a guiding principle: "We have to make buying music as easy as stealing it."

An example of the new players is RealOne, launched on December 4, which uses MusicNet. For $9.95 a month, subscribers have access to about 75,000 songs from artists ranging from Britney Spears to Linkin Park. Each month, users get 100 song downloads and 100 song streams.

But there's a catch: RealOne's songs are accessible only on the Internet and are stored on the company's computers. At the end of the month, all the songs "expire" and users have to pay again to listen to the music. And users can't download to a portable player or burn their own CD mixes.

Pressplay, which kicked off in December, started with a database of 100,000 songs, though nothing at first from some stars. Its $9.95 monthly plan offers users 300 streams, 30 downloads that don't expire as long as you subscribe, and zero CD burns. The $24.95 platinum plan includes 1,000 streams, 100 downloads, and 20 burns.

It may be tough to charge users for less service when they're accustomed to more, for free. But record labels can never hope to survive if they simply give their music away. The companies also say that music listeners want artists to be fairly compensated, and that people will pay for fast, reliable, high-quality access to songs—something the free sites don't always offer. A recent Pew survey, though, found that when a Web site with free content began charging a fee, 86 percent of users abandoned it.

If the labels can amp up MusicNet and Pressplay to include features that music lovers can't live without, like access to a song weeks in advance of its release, the companies could thrive anew. But if the pay-for-play sites fizzle, while free sites continue to grow, the labels may find themselves facing the music.

It's All Free![3]

BY LEV GROSSMAN, ET AL.
TIME, MAY 5, 2003

James Phung saw *Phone Booth* before you did. What's more, he saw it for free, in the comfort of his private home-screening room. Phung isn't a movie star or a Hollywood insider; he's a junior at the University of Texas who makes $8 an hour at the campus computer lab. But many big-budget Hollywood movies have their North American premieres in his humble off-campus apartment. Like millions of other people, Phung downloads movies for free from the Internet, often before they hit theaters. *Phone Booth* will fit nicely on his 120-GB hard drive alongside *Anger Management*, *Tears of the Sun* and about 125 other films, not to mention more than 2,000 songs. "Basically," he says, "the world is at my fingertips."

Phung is the entertainment industry's worst nightmare, but he's very real, and there are a lot more like him. Quietly, with no sirens and no breaking glass, your friends and neighbors and colleagues and children are on a 24-hour virtual smash-and-grab looting spree, aided and abetted by the anonymity of the Internet. Every month they—or is it we?—download some 2.6 billion files illegally, and that's just music. That number doesn't include the movies, TV shows, software and video games that circulate online. First-run films turn up online well before they hit the theaters. Albums debut on the Net before they have a chance to hit the charts. Somewhere along the line, Americans—indeed, computer users everywhere—have made a collective decision that since no one can make us pay for entertainment, we're not going to.

As crimes go, downloading has a distinctly victimless feel to it—can anything this fun be wrong?—but there are real consequences. Click by click, file by file, we are tearing the entertainment industry apart. CD shipments last year were down 9 percent, on top of a 6 percent decline in 2001. A report by Internet services company Divine estimates pirates swap between 400,000 and 600,000 movies online every day. It's information-superhighway robbery.

If you ask the pirates, they'll say they're just fighting for their right to party. If you ask the suits, they'll say they're fighting for their lives. "If we let this stand, you're going to see the undoing of this society," says Jack Valenti, head of the Motion Picture Association of America (M.P.A.A.). "I didn't preside over this movie industry to see it disintegrate like the music industry." Them's fightin' words, and the battle lines are being drawn. Two landmark legal decisions last week, one in favor of the entertainment industry and one against it, will shape the way we deal with digital movies and music for years to come. The only thing left to decide is which side of those battle lines you're on.

It's easy to see why the pirates do what they do. Right now you can find thousands of free movies online if you know where to look—a glance at one popular website yields links to copies of *Holes*, *Malibu's Most Wanted* and even the Rowan Atkinson comedy *Johnny English*, which won't hit U.S. theaters until July. Just about every song ever released—as well as quite a few that haven't been—is available online for nothing more than the effort it takes to point and click. Record-industry types have a cute nickname for this phenomenon: "the celestial jukebox."

Most online piracy happens through what is called file-sharing software, such as Kazaa, Gnutella and Direct Connect, that links millions of computers to one another over the Internet. File-sharing software takes advantage of the fact that music and movies are stored as digital data—they're not vinyl and celluloid anymore, but collections of disembodied, computerized bits and bytes that can be stored or played on a computer and transmitted over the Internet as easily as e-mail. Using file-sharing software, people can literally browse through one another's digital music and movie collections, picking and choosing and swapping whatever they want. If you've never tried it, it's hard to describe how seductive it is. Start up a program like Kazaa, type in the name of your favorite rock band, and a list of song titles will instantly appear on your screen. See something you like, click on it, and it's yours. An average song might take two minutes to download to your computer if you have a broadband connection. Log on any night of the week and you'll find millions of users sharing hundreds of millions of songs, movies and more.

Ask your average high school kids if they use Kazaa, and the answer is a resounding "duh."

Ask your average high school kids if they use Kazaa, and the answer is a resounding "duh." Stewart Laperouse and Jennifer Rieger, a couple at Cy-Fair High School in Houston, log on as part of their regular after-school routine—it's the new milk and cookies. Often they do their downloading à deux, after he gets out of lacrosse practice. His collection is relatively small: 150 songs and about 50 music videos. She's the real repeat offender, with 400 pilfered tracks on her hard drive. "Who wouldn't want to do this?" Rieger says. "It's totally free and it's easy." Look for pangs of guilt and you'll get only shrugs.

This isn't how it was supposed to be. A little more than three years ago the Recording Industry Association of America (R.I.A.A.), which represents most U.S. record labels, filed suit against Napster, the granddaddy of file-sharing services, for "contributory and vicarious copyright infringement." The R.I.A.A. won;

Napster lost. A judge ordered its servers shut down. End of story?

Hardly. The file-sharing services didn't go away. They evolved, getting smarter and more decentralized and harder to shut down. Napster's network relied on a central server, an Achilles' heel that made it easier to unplug and shut down. But Kazaa, now the most popular file-sharing software, is built around a floating, distributed network of individual PCs that has no center. There's no single plug to pull. Kazaa has savvily chosen a decentralized business strategy too: it's a mirage of complicated partnerships with the official owner, Sharman Networks, tucked away on the South Pacific island of Vanuatu. So far, its diffuse structure has kept its management off U.S. soil and out of U.S. courtrooms.

What we have here is not a failure to communicate; it's a raging, runaway success.

It isn't just the file-sharing companies that are evolving; the Internet is too. Broadband Internet access has become cheaper and more widespread—analysts expect the number of households with broadband to jump 41 percent this year—and that means we can move bigger, fatter files in less and less time. Personal computers have also evolved. In 1992 the average hard drive was 120 megabytes. Now it's 40 gigabytes, 300 times as big—perfect for stashing whole libraries of audio and video. CD and DVD burners used to be expensive peripherals; now they come standard. Every new PC is a self-contained entertainment studio, right out of the box. What we have here is not a failure to communicate; it's a raging, runaway success.

The consequence of the high-tech evolution is a new generation of technologically empowered consumers for whom free entertainment isn't a windfall, it's a basic right. Just ask Sean Farrell, a senior at Yale. A sophisticated listener, he dabbles in jazz and classical along with the usual hip-hop. But he hasn't bought a CD in four years. Instead, he has 5,000 songs on his computer's 430-GB hard drive, and more in the 20-GB MP3 player—an Apple iPod—that is permanently attached to his hip. When he and his roommates have parties, they don't bother with CDs, they just run cables from the computer in Farrell's bedroom to the stereo in the common room and blast the free tunes straight off his PC. "I don't feel really guilty," he says. "The music industry has to realize that this is here to stay; it's not going away." See the pattern yet?

For years people wondered whether all this downloading would actually affect the entertainment industry's bottom line. Now that last year's numbers are in, we have the answer. According to Nielsen SoundScan, CD album sales slid from 712 million units in 2001 to 680 million in 2002. CD sales in the first quarter of 2003 were down 15 million units from last year. Or look at it this way: in 2000 the top 10 albums in America sold 60 million copies; in 2001,

40 million; in 2002, 33 million. Nobody knows for sure exactly how much of the decline is caused by piracy, but it's safe to say the answer is somewhere between "some of it" and "most of it." Sure, the economy had a down year, but people found enough spare change in their couches to boost sales of MP3 players 56 percent over 2001. And while consumers bought about 680 million albums last year, they purchased 1.7 billion blank CDs—up 40 percent from the year before. The clear implication: users are downloading free music and burning it onto blank CDs. Industry analysts are reduced to fairy-tale metaphors to describe the change. The genie is out of the bottle. Pandora's box is open. The dikes have burst, and the Dutch boy has gone surfing.

Which isn't to say music executives are sitting around wringing their hands. It takes time for any corporation to recognize that its universe has changed, and major labels don't exactly turn on a dime. For Martin Bandier, chairman and CEO of EMI Music Publishing, the dime dropped three years ago when his 11-year-old son Max gave him a present: his 100 favorite Motown songs. "I said, 'But we have hundreds of copies!'" Bandier recalls. "He said, 'This is in a different place—on my hard drive.' It was scary." Bandier immediately convened a war council to figure out how to protect EMI's precious song catalog, which ranges from Judy Garland to Norah Jones. "People did not think it was real in the beginning," he says. "It's as real as can be."

Reality bit, and deep. In 2001 EMI brought in new top management, including chairman of EMI Recorded Music Alain Levy, to help navigate the brave new digital world. The administration promptly laid off 1,800 employees (20 percent of EMI's staff), which helped absorb the impact when sales fell 10 percent in 2002—and created an executive position, global head of antipiracy. It also brought in executive vice president John Rose, an e-commerce ace from consulting firm McKinsey. "The fundamental premise of hiring someone like me," says Rose, "is that this industry needs to be re-engineered." Since last summer, EMI has been holding weekly three-hour lunch meetings with artists, managers, agents and lawyers, a dozen at a time, to explain to them, as Rose puts it, "how the world needs to evolve."

First order of business: evolve some claws. Some labels (they're reluctant to identify themselves) hire professional counterhackers, companies like Overpeer, based in Manhattan, that specialize in electronic countermeasures such as "spoofing"—releasing dummy versions of popular songs onto file-sharing networks. To your average Kazaa user they look like the real thing, but when you download them, they turn out to be unplayable. Movie studios, meanwhile, staff screenings with ushers wearing night-vision goggles to suss out would-be pirates with camcorders. When Epic Records distributed review copies of the new Pearl Jam album last fall, it sent them inside CD players that had been glued shut. The

White Stripes went further: review copies of their new album *Elephant* were sent on good old-fashioned vinyl, which is trickier to copy. In the copy-protection wars, low tech is the new high tech.

For EMI, the plan is not to prohibit copying, just to keep us from doing it quite so much. In theory, the CD of the future will be smart enough to let its owner make one copy of a song for the computer, one for the iPod, and maybe burn an extra for the car, but that's it. But even that might annoy consumers who are used to making as many copies as they want. Even if the smart CD of the future becomes a reality, to work at all it will have to work absolutely perfectly. If just one copy leaks onto Kazaa, anywhere in the world, millions of people can have all the copies they want.

Of course, there's an even older-fashioned way to keep people from stealing your stuff. It's called the law. "What we're dealing with is thievery, plain and simple," says the M.P.A.A.'s Valenti. "People try to use a lot of sophistry to get away from that fact." The legal landscape on which the war against piracy will be fought is being defined right now. In January a federal judge ruled that Verizon, a telephone company that is also an Internet service provider (ISP), must honor the R.I.A.A. subpoena to reveal the identity of one of its customers, a Kazaa user whom they suspect of downloading more than 600 songs. Verizon asked for a stay of the decison, and a flurry of briefs from the M.P.A.A. (backing the record companies) and numerous privacy and consumer organizations (on behalf of Verizon) ensued. On Thursday, the judge denied Verizon's request. Unless it can get a reprieve from an appeals court, the company has 14 days (and counting) to come up with the name.

If you're going to download music, don't expect to hide behind the anonymity of the Internet.

The message is clear: If you're going to download music, don't expect to hide behind the anonymity of the Internet. On the other hand, if you're in the business of making file-sharing software, you have a lot less to worry about. On Friday a federal judge ruled that two companies—Grokster and StreamCast Networks, which makes a program called Morpheus—were not liable if users of their file-sharing software infringed on someone else's copyright. In his decision Judge Stephen Wilson cited the legal fuss that sprang up in the 1980s over Sony's Betamax technology. Like file sharing, it was a tool that could be used for both legal and illegal copying. Then, as now, the former was deemed to outweigh the latter.

The ruling is a stinging blow for the R.I.A.A. and the M.P.A.A., which brought the suit (and will appeal it), and it tells us a lot about how the war against piracy will be fought. If file-sharing services won't sit still and be sued, individual users will make easier targets. Case in point: lawsuits filed last month against students at Princeton, Michigan Technological University and Rensselaer Polytechnic Institute that seek billions of dollars in damages—$150,000 for each pirated song. Nobody thinks piracy can be stopped by suing one user at a time, but if companies focus on major uploaders—people who make huge numbers of files available for others to download—a few high-profile busts may scare off some of the rest. "In the Verizon case, we got the judgment that we really needed," says Andrew Lack, chairman and CEO of Sony Music Entertainment, "which is that on an individual basis you are being ripped off, and you have a right to stop that."

The pace is picking up as Big Media head to court with everybody they can think of. The M.P.A.A. is wrangling with a company called 321 Studios over the legality of one of 321's products, software that enables consumers to make free copies of movies from DVDs. The FBI busted a Los Angeles man last week for camcording movies off the big screen and selling copies—a legal first. Universal Music Group and EMI have even filed suit against venture-capital firm Hummer Winblad just because it invested in Napster back in 2000.

But the legal fight is far from a sure thing. Copyright laws are slippery and subjective—the judge in the Grokster case made a special plea in his ruling asking Congress to fix gaps in the laws that cover file sharing. Enforcing those laws is also tricky. Colleges, where a lot of the downloading goes on, like to think of themselves as bastions of privacy and free speech, not copyright police. The international reach of the Internet makes enforcement even dodgier. Case in point: in 1999 Jon Johansen, a Norwegian teenager, figured out how to break the copy protection on commercial DVDs, making possible the cheap, high-quality, à la carte copying of movies. This information became, shall we say, fairly popular on the Internet, earning Johansen, who was 15 at the time, the nickname "DVD Jon." In 2000 Norwegian prosecutors, egged on by the M.P.A.A., charged him with violating digital-security laws. In January the verdict came in: Johansen got off. An appeals hearing is scheduled for December.

There's another problem with suing people: it doesn't make you popular with your customers—and Big Media are already fighting a major P.R. battle. Everybody who has ever watched VH1's "Behind the Music" has heard musicians bad-mouth their record labels, and no one is going to feel bad for ripping off the suits who ripped off their favorite rock star. File sharing has become cool, a way to fight the power, to stick it to the Man. Re-engineering the public image of studio executives probably isn't in the cards—these are, after all, the same companies that coughed up $143 million last October to settle a class action accusing them of price fixing—but in the past few months, more and more artists have begun speaking out, and they stand a better chance of winning sympathy. For years musicians and other artists were reluctant to address file sharing, in part because they saw how uncool Metallica's James Hetfield looked when he tried. But in September the likes of Nelly, the Dixie Chicks, Brian Wilson and the incontrovertibly cool Missy Elliott delivered televised antipiracy scoldings. In April, Ben

There for the Taking

Here's a sampling of what's available on Kazaa at any given time, day or night.*

Television
One episode of *The Simpsons*
Download time: 18 min.
Cost on DVD: $37

Software
Warcraft III: Reign of Chaos
Download time: 1 hr. 6 min.
Cost: $32

Music
The White Stripes, "Seven Nation Army"
Download time: 2 min.
Cost on CD: $14

Movies
A Beautiful Mind
Download time: 10 hr. 3 min.
Cost on DVD: $26

*Download times using a DSL phone line

Affleck appeared in an antipiracy spot on behalf of the movie industry. Still, you don't have to be Alanis Morissette to spot the irony in a zillionaire celebrity pleading for sympathy. After a spoofed version of Madonna's new album, *American Life*, started circulating on the Net, featuring a recording of the Material Girl saying "What the f___ do you think you're doing?," a hacker took over the singer's website, Madonna.com, and posted real, downloadable MP3s of every song on the album.

The entertainment industry's grand plan for surviving piracy isn't just about the stick; there's a carrot too, a big one. The Internet offers a whole new way of selling music, and when music and movie executives are not expressing their outrage over downloading, they are salivating over a potentially massive revenue opportunity. There are already a couple of dozen legal, pay-to-play downloading services, including Pressplay, Listen.com's Rhapsody and MusicNet. Apple Computer has a new service, which was slated for rollout this Monday, that's meant to integrate seamlessly with its iPod MP3 player and its iTunes music software. Movie and TV downloading websites are sprouting up as well. Movielink, which is backed by five major Hollywood studios, made its debut in November and features a library of more than 300 films. SoapCity.com offers online episodes of daytime serials.

But these services face competition you wouldn't wish on Bill Gates. Unlike, say, Kazaa, they have to clear each song or movie or show for digital distribution with each individual artist and studio. They have made significant progress—Pressplay, for example, has upwards of 300,000 tracks available for download, with membership starting at $9.95 a month—but it's slow work. The for-pay services also mire users in a mesh of restrictions that limit what they can do with the music they download. That $9.95 plan at Pressplay buys you unlimited downloads, but you can't move the songs to your portable MP3 player or burn copies of them onto a CD, and you can listen to them only so long as you're a Pressplay subscriber. Miss a payment, and the files lock up. For $8 more a month, Pressplay gives you 10 "portable" downloads that are free of those constraints. But compare that with the roughly infinite number of unrestricted, unconstrained, infinitely copyable downloads that Kazaa offers for roughly nothing, and you can see that Pressplay has an uphill battle on its hands.

You can't have an information economy in which all information is free.

Pressplay and the other "legitimate" music services are more reliable than Kazaa and its ilk. For one thing, there's no porn and no spoofing, and Apple's new offering is expected to give the whole process a more streamlined, user-friendly feel. These services also give customers the peace of mind that comes with not breaking the law. It will be interesting to see how much that's worth. But for now listeners are staying away in droves; industry analysts estimate that the legitimate downloading services have fewer than 300,000 users in all. Still, if the retail-music business is going to survive, this may be what it has to look like, and for the business side, that's the real significance of the digital revolution. "It's not piracy per se but a transition to a digital world that will transform what a record company is and how it works," says EMI's Rose. "While downloading is an important issue, it's just symbolic of a much more fundamental shift in how music will be moved and acquired by consumers and be used."

Can the for-pay services compete? Maybe. Can antipiracy laws be enforced? Perhaps. Can copy protection stand up to a hacker army of teenage Jon Johansens? It's possible. But all this raises an interesting question: What if the pirates win? If you play the thought experiment out to its logical extreme, the body count is high. After all, you can't have an information economy in which all information is free. The major music labels would disappear; ditto the record stores that sell their CDs. The age of millionaire rock stars would be over; they would become as much a historical curiosity as the landed aristocracy is today. Instead, musicians would scratch out a living on the touring circuit, since in an age of free music the only commodity they would control is live performance, along with any merchandise they could hawk in the parking lot after the show. Hollywood would also take a hit. People might still pay to watch movies in the theater—viewing on the big screen beats

To Pay or to Pirate?

Many paths may lead to the music or movies you want, but you'll have to navigate the sometimes blurry ethical and legal traps along the way.

Buy at store

How It's Done The old fashioned way. Go to the store, pay your money, get your music or video on a disc

The Good It's a guilt-free, no-risk transaction, and you get whatever goodies the product comes with

The Bad It's expensive, you have to drive to the store (or pay for shipping), and the selection is limited

Buy download

How It's Done Visit one of the many for-pay websites and download or stream music or movies to your computer

The Good You only pay for the songs or movies you want, and you know the artists are being compensated

The Bad They may not have what you want, it's still not cheap, and many services place restrictions on use

Buy pirated disc

How It's Done Walk down the street in Any City, U.S.A., and look for the guy with the card table full of CDs and DVDs

The Good It's cheap—$10 for a DVD, less for a CD—and pirates have first-run movies while they're still in theaters

The Bad You're ripping off the artists, and the quality is often atrocious

Copy disc from friend

How It's Done Your buddy has a movie or an album you want and the technology to burn you a free copy. What are friends for?

The Good The price is right, and the quality is high. And hey, you're not the one going to hell, right?

The Bad You might be the one going to hell

Download free

How It's Done Install free file-sharing software such as Kazaa on your computer, then just head online and search for what you want

The Good All the free music, video and software you can download

The Bad You have to wade through porn and other garbage to get what you want. And the price is high: your clear conscience

watching movies on your computer—but Hollywood would have to do without revenue from video stores. Who's going to rent what they can download for free? TV studios would likewise have to do without their cushy syndication deals, since the Net would become the land of infinite reruns. Hope you like product placement—you'll be seeing a lot of it. Already this July the WB network and Pepsi plan to launch an "American Bandstand"–style TV show called "Pepsi Smash," featuring performances by big-ticket music acts. Alternative revenue streams never tasted so good.

In a sense, the future is already here. You can see it in action in Asia. Piracy is a growing phenomenon in the U.S., but in some developing countries, it is a fact of life. There's a marketplace in Karachi, Pakistan, where you can buy a DVD of *How to Lose a Guy in 10 Days* for 100 rupees (about $1.75) even while it's playing in first-run theaters in the U.S. Karachi boasts five optical-disc factories, just one of which churns out 40 million pirated discs a year. If you think American teenagers are guiltless, file-swapping punks, try talking to a Karachi shopkeeper. "We make copy of everything!" says Mohammed Haris. "Even George Bush cannot dare to come over here. We will keep the original and send his copy back home."

This kind of commercial piracy has devastated the Asian entertainment industry. In China, where piracy rates for movies, music and software are all more than 90 percent, record companies trying to develop local talent have bled money for years. Every time they try to build up a star, the pirates siphon off the profits. "There's no point in spending money to drive demand," says Samuel Chou, Warner Music's CEO for China and Taiwan, "because what you drive all goes to piracy."

It's a scary cautionary tale—but at this point, hypothetical horror stories are almost beside the point. The people have spoken, and they say they want a revolution. File sharing isn't going to save us from corporate entertainment the way the Beatles saved Pepperland from the Blue Meanies, but if it allows more people to listen to more music in more ways than they ever have before, can it be all bad? And does good or bad even matter? Technology has a way of sweeping aside questions of what is right or wrong and replacing them with the reality of what is possible. Recorded entertainment has gone from an analog object to a disembodied digital spirit roaming the planet's information infrastructure at will, and all the litigation and legislation in the world won't change it back. The genie is out of the bottle, and we're fresh out of wishes.

A New Tactic in the Download War[4]

BY DAVID SEGAL
THE WASHINGTON POST, AUGUST 21, 2002

The first time Travis Daub got "spoofed," he figured faulty software was to blame. Hoping to sample the new album by Moby, he downloaded one of its songs, "We Are All Made of Stars," from the Web site LimeWire.com. But what wound up on his hard drive wasn't what he expected.

"It was just 20 seconds of the song, repeated over and over," says Daub, a 26-year-old design director who lives in Arlington. "At first I thought it was a glitch. Then I realized someone had posted this on purpose."

The identity of that someone is a mystery—Moby's label and management team say it wasn't them. But in recent weeks, scads of "spoof" files have been anonymously posted to the hugely popular sites where music fans illegally trade songs online. Spoofs are typically nothing more than repetitive loops or snippets filled with crackle and hiss, and thousands are now unwittingly downloaded every day from file-sharing services, like Kazaa and Morpheus, that sprang up after Napster's demise.

Record labels are reluctant to discuss spoofing, but their trade group, the Recording Industry Association of America, has called it a legitimate way to combat piracy. And at least one company acknowledges that it has been hired to distribute spoofs, although it won't say by whom.

All of this suggests that the dummy files are part of a second front in the record industry's war against illegal music copying. For years, the fight focused on Web sites and their owners. Now it's starting to focus on the fans themselves.

For the labels, any anti-piracy campaign that targets consumers is risky, since it could alienate many who also spend heavily on store-bought discs. But given a two-year slide in CD sales that the industry says has cost it billions, many executives and artists believe they don't have a choice. New file-sharing ventures sprout all the time, and 2 billion songs a month are now traded online, according to the RIAA, far more than during Napster's heyday. Meantime, sales of blank CDs, which can be used to copy songs on the cheap, are skyrocketing.

So labels are racing to develop uncopyable CDs and—if indeed they're behind the spoofs—employing guerrilla tactics that complicate the unlawful uploading and downloading of songs. The labels are also supporting a bill, now under consideration in Congress, that would make it legal to "impair the operation of peer-to-peer" networks, such as LimeWire. That could be done, for example, by overloading file-sharing services with so many requests that they slow to a crawl.

"I think in the history of the music business, we've been, with regard to enforcing our rights, pretty generous with consumers," said Hilary Rosen, chairwoman of the RIAA. "But we're looking for a way to stop gross infringers, and there are measures we can take to prevent people from making 100 copies or uploading CDs for millions to take."

The strategy has generated plenty of skepticism, however, and not just among those who regard music thievery as a sacred mission. Some executives in the online music world say the majors—Sony, Universal, Warner Bros., BMG and EMI—are wasting their time. Foolproof locks, they say, don't exist in the digital realm, where it takes just one dedicated hacker to open the vault for everyone else.

Foolproof locks . . . don't exist in the digital realm, where it takes just one dedicated hacker to open the vault for everyone else.

"All this smacks of desperation," says Eric Garland, president of BigChampagne, a company hired by major labels to measure online file-sharing traffic. "When you've got a consumer movement of this magnitude, when tens of millions of people say, 'I think CD copying is cool and I'm within my rights to do it,' it gets to the point where you have to say uncle and build a business model around it rather than fight it."

Sounding a Sour Note

The record labels have been spurred to action by figures they find terrifying: The number of "units shipped"—CDs sent to record stores or directly to consumers—fell by more than 6 percent last year, and it's widely expected to fall 6 to 10 percent more by the end of 2002. Those drops are already hitting the industry hard. Labels are laying off employees, ditching artists, slashing budgets for tours and videos, and combing their back catalogues for reissues that cost almost nothing to release.

Pinpointing the cause of the sales decline is difficult. Entertainment options have multiplied in the past 20 years—the video game industry, for instance, now dwarfs the music business—giving kids a lot of new places to spend money.

There's evidence, though, that Americans are spending more time than ever listening to CDs. Market surveys suggest that more blank CDs (CD-Rs) than recorded CDs are now sold in the United States. Recorded discs still generate far more revenue, of course, since they sell for about $17 apiece, a sum that will buy about 50 CD-Rs. And CD-Rs have plenty of uses other than bootlegging music—they store photos and data, too. But analysts and retailers say the CD-R is fast replacing the cassette as the music-copying medium of choice, with sound quality that far outclasses analog tapes.

Labels claim that sales of CD-Rs spike during the same week a major new release hits stores—a sign that people are buying, say, the new Bruce Springsteen CD and making free copies of it for their friends.

Thus far, only halting, low-key steps have been taken to thwart mass copying. Just four titles, including an album by country singer Charley Pride, have been released in the United States with reconfigured coding intended to render them unplayable in computer hard drives, which is where most CD burning and uploading to Web sites takes place. Even these tentative moves proved controversial, however, because buyers who merely wanted to play the CDs on their computers couldn't do so. And one congressman said the labels warning consumers that the discs didn't play on PCs were so small that he threatened legislation.

***"The labels run the risk of angering millions of their best customers with these copy-protected CDs."*—Rep. Rick Boucher, D-Virginia**

"The labels run the risk of angering millions of their best customers with these copy-protected CDs," Rep. Rick Boucher, a Virginia Democrat and Internet policy maven, said in a recent phone interview. "That's a business call on their part. But I think there's a role for Congress to make sure that copy-protected CDs are adequately labeled."

For the labels, this first stab at safeguarding had an even greater liability: It didn't work very well. Hackers gleefully reported that they could defeat the security encryption with a felt-tip pen, and artists declined to release copy-protected albums, figuring that the discs would annoy fans without plumping their royalty checks. "It just doesn't work," said David Bowie, whose latest album, *Heathen*, was released protection-free. "I mean, what's the point?"

The majors seem to appreciate that these initial experiments were flawed. Though mum about upcoming releases with protection, they say they're back in the lab, hoping to devise software that allows legal copying (for personal use, such as a copy for the car), while blocking illegal activity (like sharing a song with millions of other fans on Napster-like services).

The ultimate goal is to retire the so-called "Red Book" CD standard that was developed in 1980 by Sony and Phillips, and which is embedded in nearly every recorded compact disc sold today. The Red Book CD was one of the most successful entertainment products in history, but unlike the DVD, it was designed without virtual security bolts. Labels won't abandon the good old five-inch plastic disc—it's a medium that consumers clearly love—but in the coming two or three years, they'll phase in new and more secure audio standards.

"What we'll see is new media coming out that will have a lot of flexibility built into the format," said Larry Kenswil of Universal Music Group.

It's unclear, though, if labels can win a spy-vs.-spy game of technology upgrades against hardware manufacturers and hackers. On the market already are devices like the Ripflash. Plug the $179 gadget into your stereo and it will convert anything that plays over your speakers—an LP, a cassette, a CD—into an MP3 file, the software format of choice for online song swappers.

"If you play it, we can record it in MP3," says Bob Fullerton of Pogo Products, which makes Ripflash. "And there's no legal way to restrict that, that I know of."

***"Kids are consuming music, it's just that they're doing it in ways that aren't making money for the industry."*—David Pakman, Senior VP at BeMusic**

Digital Do-It-Yourselfers

In the past, whenever consumers swooned for a new music format, like CDs, the record industry made a fortune from the conversion. This time, millions of listeners are again getting their music in a new medium—MP3s and other modem-friendly formats—but the labels aren't profiting from the revolution. This time the revolution is actually hurting them.

"Kids are consuming music, it's just that they're doing it in ways that aren't making money for the industry," says David Pakman, a senior vice president with Bertelsmann's BeMusic, the company's Internet music division. "Kids are saying, 'We want music, but we want it on different terms.'"

To a large extent, those terms were shaped by Napster, an early Internet star that drew millions of fans before being sued and shut down by the labels. Some of the terms are simply impossible for the industry to meet. Competing against Kazaa and Morpheus on price can't be done, since those sites don't charge a cent.

Then again, the labels have largely ignored consumer demand for song-at-a-time buying. CD singles are being phased out, apparently to push consumers to the far more profitable full-length CD. And the labels have only recently allowed subscribers to their pay-to-play Web sites, like Pressplay, to burn music onto discs.

"They've got a promotional system designed to implant a 30-second hook in your head, but it's difficult to buy just that song," said Garland of BigChampagne. "That's like Coke advertising cans on TV but selling only 12-packs in stores."

The industry counters that even if fans don't like their buying options, swiping songs isn't justified. "If I wanted to buy pants and the store will only sell it as part of a suit, I'm not allowed to steal the pants just because I'm [ticked] off," says the RIAA's Rosen.

Fans like Travis Daub don't think of themselves as shoplifters. He's running afoul of the law by downloading from LimeWire, but he's also the sort of regular CD buyer that labels adore. "I use it like radio," Daub says of the Internet. "It's easier to get hooked on an artist via MP3s."

It's getting harder now. Daub says that recent searches for an Eminem song turned up hundreds of hits that were obviously "spoofs," making it nearly impossible to find non-spoofed copies.

That delights Marc Morgenstern, CEO of Overpeer, a company that specializes in spreading spoof files over the Internet. Morgenstern is diplomatically tight-lipped: He won't disclose the names of his clients, nor will he discuss Overpeer's methods.

"We use various methods of disguise," he said. "When someone clicks on our file, they're not getting an illegal file. They receive what our clients want them to receive."

Spoofing is hardly a permanent solution to the file-sharing problem. The most downloaded album in Internet history—the recently released *The Eminem Show*—is also the best-selling album of the year, which suggests that at least some fans were spurred to buy the disc even though they already had it stashed on their hard drives. At best, spoofing is an annoyance and one that some file-sharing sites are already working to outsmart through user rating systems that, in theory, will relegate unlistenable files to the bottom of search lists.

Long-term solutions to piracy, say experts, won't come through hurdles dreamed up by techies but in authorized Web sites and technology so irresistible, so loaded with extras and so convenient that it's more appealing than anything offered by rivals.

"They'll come up with a compelling model, but the question is whether it will be compelling enough to win back consumers," said Orin Herskowitz of the Boston Consulting Group, a consulting firm. "If they just sue and hassle people without an alternative, they'll eventually lose."

That might leave money in the pocket of Travis Daub that otherwise might have been spent on music. "I lost interest in that particular song," he says of his unhappy attempt to listen to the Moby tune. "And I didn't buy the album, either."

Make Copyright Law User-Friendly[5]

BY PAUL BRENNAN
COMPUTER WEEKLY, NOVEMBER 7, 2002

"I am constantly faced with complex arguments as to why a particular incidence of copying software is not illegal in those circumstances," writes the Federation Against Software Theft's Paul Brennan.

However, when an employee takes source code, or a company removes protection from a demo version of software and sells it as its own product, it certainly feels like theft, but technically it is not stealing. The case of *Oxford v. Morris* held that software was not property and copying it was not stealing for the purpose of the Theft Act. However, it is copyright infringement.

So how do we go about clarifying matters and increasing protection for software publishers? Outlined below are various significant measures that are either in progress—or need to happen—to ensure the huge progress made in software licensing laws made over the past 20 years does not fall by the wayside.

Harmonisation

Many directives have come through from the European Union (EU), including the Copyright Directive—now the EU is turning its attention to enforcement. Soon we will see the draft Enforcement Directive that will harmonise laws in the various countries. Harmonisation is important as it ensures a crime is the same in all countries.

Defrauding

Recommended by the Law Commission, and awaiting the Government to put it into legislation, a statutory Offence to Defraud will make it an offence to take software with an intention to cheat and deceive. It will remove the need for the prosecution's currently time-consuming process of dealing with technical copyright points.

Technical measures

More and more software publishers are using technical measures to protect their software but there is always the risk that it is removed or circumvented. Although the new Copyright Directive that comes into force in the UK in December provides some

5. Article for *Computer Weekly* by Paul Brennan, General Counsel of Federation Against Software Theft (FAST), author of *Law for IT Professionals*, EMIS, UK, 2003, ISBN 1 85811 322 9.

enhanced safeguards, the downside is that they do not apply to software as, for no logical reason that I can see, software was specifically excluded from this benefit. This needs to be rectified.

The Federation Against Software Theft's (FAST's) greater concern is that the present UK draft regulations do not allow criminal penalties for circumvention of technical protection, and civil penalties can be expensive. If circumvention of technical protection was a criminal offence even a developer starting out would be able to go down to the local police station and expect something to be done rather than having to take out an expensive injunction. (One small software publisher recently spent £25,000 in two months on a case).

In 1994 Parliament passed Section 107A Copyright Designs and Patent Act 1988 to give trading standards the authority and duty to protect copyright items such as software. However, eight years later it has still not received the necessary commencement order to make it law.

Punishment

Compared to the US, damages in the UK for copyright infringement are low, seemingly relying on costs as the penalty. Crime in the 21st century cannot be fought with a 19th-century system. Too often everyone involved in the case suffers and the software house gets a further hammering.

Proof

A copyright case can entail proving—at great length, expense and detail—"the bleeding obvious," to paraphrase Monty Python. This is especially so in criminal matters where no presumptions are allowed. Even in cases of flagrant breach there are too many technical defenses available—it needs to be simplified.

Searches

Search orders are hand-crafted, expensive and complicated. For instance, an independent solicitor from a different firm must attend the search to explain his or her rights to the defendant. This adds yet more cost, and must be simplified.

Conclusion

The present laws have come a long way and do offer protection. However, many software publishers do not see the system as user-friendly, and believe it to be expensive and a waste of their time.

The resulting failure of software publishers to pursue rightful claims is a worrying development in a country that needs innovation—and one that must be addressed by all of us connected with the industry.

Gauging TV's 'Net Effect[6]

BY PAIGE ALBINIAK
BROADCASTING & CABLE, FEBRUARY 21, 2000

Consumers eventually will be able to watch any TV station at any time over the Internet, most agree. The question, posed before Congress last week, is how to let the genie out of the bottle without putting content providers out of business.

While some suggestions were given to the House Telecommunications Subcommittee—such as developing technology that would limit the geographic reach of Internet broadcasts—for now the answer is protect companies' rights to control their content, let the marketplace work out distribution agreements and enforce laws that forbid Internet companies from streaming copyright content without permission.

A powerful coalition of media companies, broadcasters and sports leagues are up in arms over one tiny Internet company's attempt to stream TV signals on the Web. The site, iCraveTV.com, started streaming the signals of 17 TV stations in the Toronto market area, which includes Buffalo, N.Y., in early December. By the end of January, a Pennsylvania federal court had shut the Canada-based site down. A similar coalition of Canadian broadcasters and content providers hope to do the same in Canada.

But even with that decisive early victory, companies whose revenues are based solely on the value of their copyrights are nervous. In their view, once a digital product is placed on the Web, they have lost all control. It enters a realm where anyone can and will make perfect copies and send them all over the world.

Still, the companies aren't so worried that they want Congress to step in.

"We are not asking the Congress to do anything specific at this time," Motion Picture Association of America President Jack Valenti told the House Telecommunications Subcommittee last week. "When there is an advocacy for enlarging compulsory licenses or other congressionally mandated marketplace interventions, we recommend that the Congress remember what former Speaker Sam Rayburn once declared to be the three most important words in the congressional lexicon: 'Wait a minute.'"

6. Article by Paige Albiniak from *Broadcasting & Cable* February 21, 2000. Copyright © *Broadcasting & Cable*. Reprinted with permission.

"For now, the laws appear to be working well to permit TV broadcasters and other copyright owners to protect themselves against this new, ultra-high-tech form of piracy," said Paul Karpowicz, vice president of LIN Television Corp., which owns one of the Buffalo TV stations that iCraveTV.com was streaming.

So far, Congress agrees with that view. Congress must proceed "cautiously and deliberately," said Rep. Billy Tauzin (R-La.), chairman of the House Telecommunications Subcommittee.

But members know the time is coming when they are going to have to provide a solution to this problem and let technology take them where it will.

"It's only a matter of time before Web-based broadcasting will allow this technology to compete on an equal footing with satellite and cable," said Rep. Michael Oxley (R-Ohio).

***"We are a Canadian company run by Canadians, and we do not seek to influence the development of American copyright law."*—Ian McCallum, VP of iCraveTV.com**

For now, what broadcasters, sports leagues and media companies want is the ability to control who can distribute their products and to whom. They are not opposed to providing products on the Internet; indeed, the AOL-Time Warner merger proves that this is the direction in which the industry is headed. But they want to be paid. In their eyes, iCraveTV.com's actions amount to nothing less than stealing.

"We are not against the Internet," said Karpowicz. "But what we are against is allowing the Internet to take advantage of our copyrighted material and use it illegally to hurt us and our local viewers."

Ian McCallum, vice president of iCraveTV.com, defended his company's actions by saying that Canadian law allows Internet, cable and satellite companies to retransmit the programming of any local broadcaster, so long as the distributor pays the required blanket copyright fees. iCraveTV's service was meant only for Canadians, McCallum says, and the company did not realize that no one would abide by the "honor system" it had set up.

"We are a Canadian company run by Canadians, and we do not seek to influence the development of American copyright law," McCallum said. "However, we hope that American law will not be applied in such a way as to make it impossible for those outside the United States who want to operate under the laws of their own country and to pay a fair return to American copyright holders."

iCraveTV may be the only entity that believes it is abiding by any law: Canadian broadcasters also have filed suit in Canada against iCraveTV, demanding that it cease its actions.

Powell Preaching the Wonders of TiVo[7]

BY DAVID BLOOM AND PAMELA MCCLINTOCK
DAILY VARIETY GOTHAM, JANUARY 13, 2003

FCC topper Michael Powell loves his TiVo, calling it "god's machine" at this weekend's Consumer Electronics Show. But having the nation's top regulator touting the personal video recorder is likely to chill the hearts of TV and cable execs, who already worry the devices could render ads impotent and piracy rampant.

"TiVo is god in my household. I can't wait to walk in the house each day to see what it's recorded for me," Powell said Friday during a Q&A session with Consumer Electronics Assn. prexy-CEO Michael Shapiro.

The top regulator, a self-avowed "complete gadget freak," said the device was one of his two favorite holiday gifts (along with Microsoft's Xbox vidgame console). But his public enthusiasm comes just as TiVo is inextricably bound up in a much bigger debate over what the FCC should do to protect content in the digital age.

Powell is at the heart of that discussion, leading the commission's effort to balance the concerns of Hollywood, consumer-electronics and computer makers and consumers. TiVo and PVRs from competitors such as SonicBlue allow consumers to fast-forward through or completely skip ads from recorded programming.

Turner Broadcasting topper Jamie Kellner and Viacom's Mel Karmazin have warned that U.S. TV households will have to start paying for broadcast programming they see today for free if TiVo keeps gaining ground. At CES, speakers said more than 2 million of the machines are now in the market, a still tiny but fast-growing fraction of the country's TV watchers.

"We give you all this great content for free, and all we ask is for you to watch our commercials," Karmazin said last year. "If the time comes when you don't watch our commercials, then we will have to make our money some other way."

Cable king Brian Roberts of Comcast says a "TiVo in the house is the Napster" of the future.

TiVo also stirs piracy concerns, because the TV industry is worried that hackers will be able to copy and distribute programs stored on the machines. SonicBlue's latest Replay PVRs are an even bigger concern (and the target of industry lawsuits), because

---

7. Article by David Bloom, Pamela McClintock from *Daily Variety Gotham* January 13, 2003.

they are connected to the Internet and allow a user to send up to 15 copies of a favored program to other Replay users, exactly what Powell told conference attendees he'd like to do with his TiVo.

"Is there a way to share a program with my sister? She loves TV as much as I do," Powell said.

Shapiro shot back, to the merriment of the audience, "It's up to you, actually."

That's what has broadcasters and cablers worried.

Clean Flicks v. Hollywood: Intellectual Property Owners Losing Control[8]

BY SCOTT W. BREEDLOVE
INTELLECTUAL PROPERTY & TECHNOLOGY LAW JOURNAL, JUNE 2003

A recent headline reported that government officials in a conservative, Islamic province of Pakistan incinerated a pile of videos and compact discs as part of a campaign to wipe out material authorities deemed obscene.

Meanwhile, back in the United States and 180 degrees away from Pakistan, Hollywood directors are looking to incinerate videos because they may *not* be obscene, anymore. The directors have asked a federal court in Colorado to order a video store to offer its feature film videos "for impound and destruction" because the video store edited the directors' films to "sanitize" portions that the store's customers find objectionable.[1]

Filed in August and not yet to the discovery stage, the Colorado case (known as *Clean Flicks* after the primary video chain involved) will explore fundamental intellectual property issues in the copyright and Lanham Act areas. The issues concern how much control an author of, or the owner of a copyright in, a creative work may exercise once he or she has put that work in the stream of commerce. The case should offer lessons on the limitations of intellectual property rights after the first sale.

Background on the Clean Flicks Litigation

Clean Flicks and numerous similar video stores buy well-known feature film videos, remove or modify objectionable material, and then sell or rent the modified videos to their customers. Neither the directors of the movies nor the film studios that own the copyrights in the movies authorize the modifications. The question is whether authorization is necessary.

Clean Flicks apparently makes no attempt to disguise the fact that it has modified the movies in its stores. Indeed, sanitizing movies is Clean Flicks' business. That is presumably the reason its customers go to Clean Flicks instead of Blockbuster. Clean Flicks claims in its pleadings that its business "involves targeting a new

8. Reprinted with permission from Aspen Publishers, © 2003, Scott W. Breedlove, *Intellectual Property and Technology Law Journal*, "*Clean Flicks v. Hollywood*: Intellectual Property Owners Losing Control," Volume 15, Number 6, June 2003, 6–11, *www.aspenpublishers.com.*

audience beyond the audience of the original work. This new audience are individuals who are not members of the original audience because the work contains material they, the new audience, find objectionable."[2] Given this business model, it is not surprising that Clean Flicks also says that its edited versions are clearly labeled as content-edited, both on the packaging and in the presentation.

The Hollywood directors, believing their reputations to be at stake, appear incensed that someone would edit sex scenes, violence, and curse words out of their creations. The Directors Guild of America issued a press release soon after the *Clean Flicks* case was filed. Its president summarized the Directors Guild's position: "It is wrong to cut scenes from a film—just as it is to rip pages from a book—simply because we don't like the way something was portrayed or said, then resell it with the original title and creator's name still on it."[3] The directors, who seem to suggest that their name should not even be mentioned in connection with a sanitized film, are not creators of low-grade pornos, either. The directors specifically named in the *Clean Flicks* litigation include Steven Spielberg, Martin Scorsese, Robert Redford, Sydney Pollack, Irwin Winkler, and Betty Thomas.

***"It is wrong to cut scenes from a film—just as it is to rip pages from a book."*—Jack Shea, President, Directors Guild of America**

These directors, however, are not the copyright owners; so they are looking beyond U.S. copyright laws to protect what are essentially moral rights in their creative works. While moral rights, recognized outside the United States, do not enjoy express protection within, a line of cases under § 43(a) of the Lanham Act provides at least a glimmer of hope for the directors' legal position.

The movie studios, as the copyright owners, also have joined the Clean Flicks lawsuit. Their involvement will test the limits of the fair-use defense to copyright infringement.

Copyright Infringement or Good, Clean Fair Use?

A number of techniques are available for Clean Flicks to sanitize Hollywood's movies. At least some of them involve copying the original videotape onto another tape where the edits are made.[4] Because reproduction is among the bundle of rights included in a copyright, the studios should have a *prima facie* case of copyright infringement respecting these editing techniques. This is so even though the first sale doctrine applies to Clean Flicks' distribution of videos generally. In other words, copyright law clearly permits Clean Flicks to sell or rent the videos it purchases, but the first sale doctrine does not necessarily apply to copying the videos or modifying them before the re-sale.[5]

That is not the end of the analysis, of course. Section 107 of the Copyright Act provides that certain otherwise infringing acts are fair uses that will not be condemned as copyright infringement.

The fair-use defense was a judicial creation. It recognizes that a copyright is, in the United States at least, more for public good than private benefit. The U.S. Supreme Court has explained that "copyright law, like the patent statutes, makes reward to the owner a secondary consideration. . . . It is said that reward to the author or artist serves to induce release to the public of the products of his creative genius."[6] To give the public appropriate access to the creative works of authors, then, Congress has limited the author's monopoly. The bottom line for intellectual property owners such as the movie studios in the Clean Flicks case is this: Copyright protection in the United States has never granted the copyright owner "complete control over all possible uses of his work."[7]

The *Clean Flicks* court therefore will need to decide whether Clean Flicks' reproduction of the movies in a modified form is a fair use outside the scope of the copyright monopoly. Section 107 provides a non-exhaustive list of the factors that the court should consider in making the evaluation. That evaluation will not be simple. As a well-known copyright treatise puts it:

> One case calls this obscure doctrine of fair use "the most troublesome in the whole law of copyright." Another notes that the "doctrine is entirely equitable and is so flexible as virtually to defy definition." Nonetheless, fair use is unique in that the U.S. Supreme Court has repeatedly addressed its contours. Whereas the vast majority of copyright issues remain unaddressed by the nation's highest tribunal, landmark decisions from 1984, 1985, and 1994 treat fair use at great length. The malleability of fair use emerges starkly from the fact that all 3 cases were overturned at each level of review, 2 of them by split opinions at the Supreme Court level.[8]

As has often been true in other copyright litigation, "undoubtedly the single most important" and "central" factor in evaluating Clean Flicks' use will be the fourth statutory factor: "The effect of the use upon the potential market for or value of the copyrighted work."[9] The market effect in the *Clean Flicks* case most directly addresses the fundamental goal of copyright to ensure broad public access to creative works. That (1) the use at issue may be commercial, (2) the nature of the work is creative entertainment, and (3) the reproduction is nearly 100 percent hardly seems to impact whether Clean Flicks' use is fair. At most, the first three factors simply suggest that the feature films are very worthy of copyright protection, and the court should carefully consider how Clean Flicks' copying affects the market incentives that drive creativity in this country.

Perhaps the most important fact about Clean Flicks' copying is that it is limited to one (modified) copy for each original that Clean Flicks buys. Using any of the Clean Flicks methodologies, Clean Flicks' use does not seem to increase the number of customers who can take possession, whether through purchase or rental, of the movie.[10] Thus, Clean Flicks does not buy one original and then make 10 copies to avoid buying more originals. Clearly, *that* would be unfair. Authors would have almost no economic incentive to create if one sale of their work would generate enough unauthorized copies to satisfy the demands of the entire consuming public. This sort of scheme would temporarily increase the public's access to creative works, but it would be sure to dry up the creation of works and ultimately devastate the public good. A "use that has no demonstrable effect upon the potential market for, or the value of, the copyrighted work need not be prohibited in order to protect the author's incentive to create. The prohibition of such non-commercial uses would merely inhibit access to ideas without any countervailing benefit."[11]

The Supreme Court's analysis in the landmark 1984 fair-use decision in *Sony v. Universal City Studios*[12] applies to Clean Flicks in important ways. A critical issue in that case was whether a television viewer could copy television programs without violating the copyright in those programs. The court specifically considered a hypothetical viewer's copying for purposes of time shifting, that is, copying a program simply to watch it later when the viewer's schedule permits. Stepping through the four fair use factors, the Supreme Court concluded that this sort of copying was a fair use. First, the *Sony* court emphasized that the use there was non-commercial. Though apparently distinguishing that copying from the Clean Flicks situation, the distinction turns out to be more of form than substance. If Clean Flicks' customers had the technological know-how to sanitize movies themselves, their copying toward this end would be just as non-commercial as that of the hypothetical television viewer in *Sony*. That sanitization generally requires an expert's help should not render the copying unfair any more than time shifting would suddenly become commercial if *Sony*'s hypothetical television viewer could not program a VCR and had to call in a paid professional to help. In any event, while the *Sony* court suggested that every commercial use of copyrighted material is presumptively unfair,[13] the Supreme Court's decision 10 years later in *Campbell vs. Acuff-Rose Music, Inc.*[14] clarified that no presumption is appropriate except in the case of "mere duplication for commercial purposes," that is, when the entire original is duplicated to serve as a "market replacement for [the original], making it likely that cognizable market harm to the original will occur."[15] That sort of commercial duplication would occur if Clean Flicks copied one original *Titanic* tape and made 100 copies to serve as market replacements to avoid buying 99 more originals.

At bottom, though, the commercial/non-commercial distinction only distracts from the complete market analysis required by the fourth factor of § 107. That analysis suggests that some of the same Hollywood studios involved in *Sony* may again be involved in self-destructive legal argument.

Clean Flicks' use . . . seems to benefit both the public and the studios.

In *Sony*, the studios feared that time-shifting television programs would reduce audiences for telecast reruns. The district court found, however, that time-shifting was more likely to help the studios than harm them; that the videotaping might allow more people to view the studio's broadcasts. The Supreme Court noted that these conclusions "are buttressed by the fact that to the extent time-shifting expands public access to freely broadcast television programs, it yields societal benefits." It therefore agreed with the district court's conclusion that the time-shifting at issue was a fair use.[16]

Clean Flicks' use also seems to benefit both the public and the studios; the public by expanding public access to popular movies, and the studios by permitting them to reap the benefit of each new viewer to whom Clean Flicks gives access to those movies. Some significant portion of Clean Flicks' customers of a sanitized movie are likely to be individuals who might not have been permitted (by their parents or their conscience, for example) to watch the movie in its unaltered state. To this extent, Clean Flicks' use analogizes closely to making a copy of a copyrighted work for the convenience of a blind person, a use "expressly identified by the House Committee Report as an example of fair use, with no suggestion that anything more than a purpose to entertain or to inform need motivate the copying."[17]

Nonetheless, expanding public access to copyrighted works would hardly seem fair if the copyright owners were not getting the corresponding benefit. Here, though, they are. Clean Flicks apparently does not seek "to profit from exploitation of the copyrighted material without paying the customary price."[18] Rather, if Clean Flicks has five customers who object to the sex scene in *Titanic* but desire to own a sanitized version, Clean Flicks must pay the customary price for five movies in order to make the five sales. Absent Clean Flicks' involvement, five fewer persons would have effective access to the copyrighted work, and the studios might make five fewer sales of the videos.

The four-factor test articulated by the Supreme Court asks whether unrestricted and widespread conduct like that of the alleged infringer would result in a substantially adverse impact on the potential market for the original work. Based on the win-win scenario that Clean Flicks' use seems to create, the answer would be no. The question gets somewhat trickier, though, because the analysis also must account for harm to the market for derivative works. Conceivably, the studios could choose to sanitize or license others to sanitize their own movies into some new derivative work, and they may argue that Clean Flicks' use harms them in this market. That argument would not be compelling here, however, even if the studios were in fact to commit to that market. One treatise notes the danger of reasoning in circular fashion that the copyright owner's potential market is to license the very use of the copyrighted work being made by the alleged infringer.[19] If Clean Flicks' use is otherwise fair, Clean Flicks should be allowed to continue sanitizing movies even if the studios later decide to compete against it in that niche market.

Given the likely benefit to the studios from Clean Flicks expanding the studios' consumer base, a concern on some other level may in fact be driving the studios to oppose Clean Flicks. *Sony* provides a basis to speculate what that concern might be. In the *Sony* trial, the studios' experts, after admitting that copying television programs solely to time-shift would not result in much harm, explained that the studios' "greatest concern about time-shifting is with 'a point of important philosophy that transcends even commercial judgment.' They fear that with any Betamax usage, 'invisible boundaries' are passed: 'The copyright owner has lost control over his program.'"[20]

That is the same philosophical point that could line the studios up against Clean Flicks. The ultimate decision in the Clean Flicks case will likely be a reminder that copyright owners should be advised (by their intellectual property counsel) of the line between what feels right and what is copyright.

Mutilation Actions and Moral Rights Under the Lanham Act

The Hollywood directors have no copyright interest in the Clean Flicks movies, but they are essentially the authors of these creative works, and their names are attached to them. With their personal investment in the movies, the directors' opposition to Clean Flicks' use graduates from the philosophical to the spiritual. The intellectual property rights they invoke through the Lanham Act, moreover, may be even more ethereal than the copyright fair-use defense.

One commentator has explained in grandiose terms the forces at work:

> Authors draw inspiration for creation from the powerful forces deep within their souls. When this inspiration becomes manifest in the form of a concrete work of authorship, that work reflects the individual spirituality and personality of the author. As such, the work embodies a concrete connection with its author and the human need for attribution symbolizes this linkage.[21]

Even the common name given to the rights that these authors seek to enforce, "moral rights," suggests a religious zeal to the arguments. Though they protect authors regardless of copyright ownership, moral rights, also known internationally as *droit moral*, are a recognized subset of copyright in many countries. The United States, however, is not among them. The very appellate decision at the heart of the directors' arguments, *Gilliam vs. American Broadcasting Companies, Inc.*, recognized that "American copyright law, as presently written, does not recognize moral rights or provide a cause of action for their violation, since the law seeks to vindicate the economic, rather than the personal, rights of authors."[22]

Gilliam and its progeny do, however, provide authors some protection under § 43(a) of the Lanham Act. Applying the Second Circuit's analysis in *Gilliam*, the Lanham Act can sometimes step in where copyright stops short to defend authors' interests.

The *Gilliam* Cause of Action

The works at issue in *Gilliam* were three 30-minute comedy programs originally written and performed by Monty Python for the British Broadcasting Corporation (BBC). In its agreement with the BBC, Monty Python had retained substantial control over the content of the programs, requiring consultation with the writers for any changes to the script that were not "minor." Nothing in the agreement permitted the BBC to alter a program once it had been recorded. Later, the BBC permitted ABC to edit and air the programs in the United States. ABC omitted approximately 27 percent of the programs, apparently to allow time for commercials and to delete offensive portions.[23] In the process, ABC distorted Monty Python's work:

> We find that the truncated version at times omitted the climax of the skits to which [Monty Python's] rare brand of humor was leading and at other times deleted essential elements in the schematic development of a storyline. We therefore agree with [the district court's] conclusion that the edited version broadcast by ABC impaired the integrity of [Monty Python's] work and represented to the public as the product of [Monty Python] what was actually a mere caricature of their talents.[24]

Perhaps the Clean Flicks movies, or some portion of them, could meet this same standard. The directors likely will argue that what Clean Flicks leaves on its cutting room floor is integral to the storyline of their films. A closer look at *Gilliam*, however, suggests the directors will face an uphill battle.

The decision in favor of Monty Python seemed to rely heavily on Monty Python's retention of artistic control in the license agreement with the BBC. First, in directing the district court to enter a preliminary injunction, the Second Circuit found a likelihood of copyright infringement in part because the editing contravened the agreement's limitation on the BBC's right to edit Monty Python material (and the BBC could not license to ABC more rights than the BBC had).[25] Then, though its decision on the copyright issue obviated any need to discuss the Lanham Act theory at that preliminary stage, the Second Circuit went on to apply it anyway. The concurring opinion suggested that the theory might not have been necessary at any stage: "If the licensee may, by contract, distort the recorded work, the Lanham Act does not come into play. If the licensee has no such right by contract, there will be a violation in breach of contract."[26]

Still, the *Gilliam* opinion reflects a high regard for artistic integrity even beyond the terms of any license agreement. While recognizing U.S. law does not provide a cause of action for a violation of an author's moral rights, the Second Circuit concluded "[n]evertheless" that artists must be able to obtain relief for mutilation of their work before the public on whom the artists depend financially. The absence of relief would, the court reasoned, undermine "the economic incentive for artistic and intellectual creation that serves as the foundation for American copyright law."[27]

The Gilliam opinion reflects a high regard for artistic integrity even beyond the terms of any license agreement.

The *Gilliam* court viewed the cause of action for mutilation as one that "finds its roots" in *droit moral*, but *Gilliam* and its limited progeny reflect at most an Americanized version of moral rights that focuses on consumers and depends on economic injury or at least the likelihood of it. The Americanized version based on § 43(a) of the Lanham Act simply cannot equate to traditional moral rights because they are focused on different interests. In the words of one commentator advocating explicit recognition in the United States of the moral right of attribution (i.e., the right of an author to be recognized as such): "Even those courts that do find in favor of a plaintiff author based on a section 43(a) violation recognize and safeguard the underlying damage to the author's spirit as a secondary concern—the primary focus always is on whether consumers are deceived through the defendant's false representations."[28]

But the moral right of integrity, that is, the author's right to prohibit misrepresentations of the author's work, seems an easier fit with § 43(a). To the extent that a person uses in commerce a name or false description of origin that is likely to confuse the public as to an author's association with or sponsorship of a particular work, that section of the Lanham Act may provide a remedy. Still, if Monty Python authored a program, ABC should be allowed to say so. ABC went astray in the Second Circuit's opinion, however, by so deforming the programs that ABC could no longer fairly represent Monty Python to be the author. Throughout its opinion, the Second Circuit, in reliance on the district court's findings at the preliminary injunction stage, labeled ABC's truncated version of Monty Python's programs "an impairment of the integrity of their programs," "a substantially altered form," "an actionable mutilation," "garbled," "distorted," and "a mere caricature of [Monty Python's] talents."[29] In a footnote, the court illustrated the extent of the distortion by describing one scene in which ABC's edits left the audience wondering why and how a character suddenly became soaking wet in the middle of a skit.

In short, *Gilliam* supports a cause of action when one deforms an author's work "to present him to the public as the creator of a work not his own, and thus make him subject to criticism for work he has not done."[30] In relying on *Gilliam*, the directors must clear the high hurdle of establishing that Clean Flicks edits the directors' feature films so substantially that the edits mutilate the films and mislead the public by associating the directors with the sanitized versions of their movies.

The directors' task seems nearly impossible given Clean Flicks' alleged business practices. Clean Flicks apparently sells itself as a company that edits movies to remove objectionable content. Clearly, the directors have lost control to some degree of the movies that they have created. Some scenes or words that the directors chose to include, whether to fulfill their artistic vision or to give the masses what they will pay to see, are getting excluded. Thus, if the law were seeking to protect some inherent moral rights "concerned primarily with safeguarding the author's dignity as both an individual and as an author,"[31] it might favor the directors. As the *Gilliam* concurrence noted, however, "the Lanham Act does not deal with artistic integrity. It only goes to misdescription of origin and the like."[32]

With its focus on a misdescription of origin, the *Gilliam* concurring opinion suggested that no Lanham Act violation would exist were ABC to clarify to the viewing audience that Monty Python did not approve ABC's version. The majority, however, believed that an explanatory legend would not be a workable solution in that case. The majority argued that the television viewers might miss the explanation if they tuned in late, and in any event, the viewers had no means to compare the truncated version with the original to determine for themselves the talents of Monty Python.[33]

Clean Flicks' business does not raise these concerns. First, Clean Flicks' customers will not likely miss the fact that Clean Flicks has edited the movies. Presumably, that is the reason that they go to Clean Flicks. It should be clear to its customers that the directors directed the movies and that Clean Flicks cleaned them. Second, these customers can certainly compare the original. Indeed, one of Clean Flicks' methods is to rent both the sanitized and the original versions to the customer.[34]

Proving a *Gilliam* Claim

District court decisions following *Gilliam* suggest that, if the district court in Colorado accepts *Gilliam*, the directors' mutilation cause of action will at least raise a factual issue, albeit one that might be appropriate for summary judgment. The fact question was a close one in *Lish vs. Harper's Magazine Foundation*,[35] for example. There, the defendant magazine had published a letter from the plaintiff without his authorization. The magazine deleted approximately 48 percent of the letter and had failed to mark any of the deletions by ellipses. The court emphasized that the author had failed to introduce any survey evidence or other objective evidence to establish that the readers of the magazine had been misled. In the face of strongly opposing expert views as to whether the letter had been garbled in the *Gilliam* sense and in the absence of any survey evidence, the district court concluded that the author had not proved that the magazine's version of the letter had substantially distorted the original.[36]

The fact question was apparently not so close in *Playboy Enterprises, Inc. vs. Dumas*.[37] An artist in that case had prepared certain works of art for a magazine. Later, the magazine reproduced some

Intellectual property owners . . . cannot always completely control their creative works in the stream of commerce.

of the art in posters, but the artist had not authorized or approved the magazine's selection or quality of the art. In addition, the magazine altered some of the art by, among other things, covering a woman's breasts. The magazine advertised that the posters were "by" the artist and "from" the magazine's collection. The court found that these representations were literally true. In addition, the court found insufficient evidence that the magazine had violated § 43(a) of the Lanham Act by altering the art. Again, the plaintiff artist offered no objective evidence to establish the reaction of the public to the alterations, which the evidence suggested were very minor. Thus, the court found insufficient evidence that the alterations on the posters had "converted or 'garbled' [the artist's] works into something new."[38]

The evidence is not yet in, but the directors probably will not be able to prove that Clean Flicks is misleading consumers by advertising that, for example, Steven Spielberg directed *Saving Private Ryan*, including the sanitized version. The directors will want to introduce surveys or other objective evidence that, despite Clean Flicks' emphasis on editing movies, its customers are misled or confused as to the origins of the films.

Conclusion

Intellectual property owners should understand that they cannot always completely control their creative works in the stream of commerce. They may, at times, need the practical advice of a proverb: The harder you squeeze, the more that slips through your fingers. *Sony* almost proved it. Had the studios won the day by proving that VCR manufacturers were contributory infringers, the studios might have missed out on the blockbuster that is the U.S. video business.

The Hollywood studios no doubt have their own reasons for opposing Clean Flicks' business, but they should consider how Clean Flicks can help them. The economics suggest that Clean Flicks' use is fair for the very reason that the studios stand to profit. In a legal system that values copyright as a public good more than a private benefit, a copyright owner's disapproval, or even disgust, with how its work is being used is not enough to support a copyright infringement action.

Likewise, authors of creative works should understand that U.S. law focuses not so much on the purity of their artistic vision as on the consumer.[39] Giving the public access to creative works often means giving up some control. So long as consumers are not misled, authors without rights in copyright or contract may have to watch while someone uses their works in ways that offend them.

Even so, companies can retain greater rights by contract when a license, rather than an outright sale, is practical. In that case, understanding the limitations of authors' rights and the breadth of fair use may inform the decision of whether and what to license.

Notes

1. *Huntsman v. Soderbergh*, Civil Action No. 02-M-1662 (D.Colo. Aug. 29, 2002) (*Clean Flicks* lawsuit), Amended Counterclaim, Prayer for Relief, ¶ (c).
2. *Id.* Second Amended Complaint and Jury Demand, ¶ 3.
3. Directors Guild of America Press Release, Sept. 20, 2002, available at *http://www.dga.org/news/pr_expand.php3?281.*
4. *Clean Flicks* Lawsuit, Second Amended Complaint and Jury Demand, ¶¶ 8, 11.
5. *See* 17 U.S.C.S. § 109(a) (Law. Co-op. Supp. 1992).
6. *Sony Corp. v. Universal City Studios, Inc.*, 464 U.S. 417, 429 (1984).
7. *Id.* at 432.
8. 4 Melville B. Nimmer et al., Nimmer On Copyright § 13.05, at 13–150 (2002).
9. 17 U.S.C.S. § 107(4) (Law. Co-op. 1994); *see* Harper & Row Publishers v. Nation Enterprises, 471 U.S. 539, 560 (1985); *Stewart v. Abend*, 495 U.S. 207, 238 (1990).
10. *See supra* n.4.
11. *Sony*, 464 U.S. at 450–451 (footnote omitted).
12. 464 U.S. 417 (1984).
13. *Id.* at 451.
14. Campbell v. Acuff-Rose Music, Inc., 510 U.S. 569 (1994).

15. *Id.* at 591.
16. *Sony*, 464 U.S. at 453–454.
17. *Id.* at 455, n.40.
18. *See Harper & Row*, 471 U.S. at 562.
19. *See* 4 Nimmer, *supra* n.8, § 13.05(A)(4), at 13–184.
20. *Sony*, 464 U.S. at 451 (quoting 480 F. Supp. 429, 467 (C.D.Cal. 1979)).
21. Roberta Rosenthal Kwall, "The Attribution Right in the United States: Caught in the Crossfire Between Copyright and Section 43(a)," 77 Wash. L. Rev. 985, 985–986 (2002) (footnote omitted).
22. Gilliam v. American Broadcasting Co., Inc., 538 F.2d 14, 24 (2d Cir. 1976).
23. *Id.* at 17–19.
24. *Id.* at 25 (footnote omitted).
25. *Id.* at 19–21.
26. *Id.* at 27.
27. *Id.* at 24.
28. Kwall, *supra* n.21, at 1020–1021.
29. *Gilliam*, 538 F.2d at 18–25.
30. *Id.* at 24.
31. Kwall, *supra* n.21, at 986.
32. *Gilliam*, 538 F.2d at 27.
33. *Id.* at 25 & n.13, 27.
34. *See supra* n.4.
35. Lish v. Harper's Magazine Foundation, 807 F. Supp. 1090 (S.D.N.Y. 1992).
36. *Id.* at 1093, 1107.
37. Playboy Enterprises, Inc. v. Dumas, 831 F. Supp. 295 (S.D.N.Y. 1993), *modified*, 840 F. Supp. 256 (S.D.N.Y. 1993), *remanded on other grounds*, 53 F.3d 549 (2d Cir. 1995).
38. *Id.* at 315–317.
39. Section 106A of the Copyright Act, granting rights of attribution and integrity to the authors of works of visual art, is an exception. See 17 U.S.C.S. § 106A (Law. Co-op. 1994).

Bibliography

Books

Berman, Bruce. *From Ideas to Assets: Investing Wisely in Intellectual Property*. New York: John Wiley & Sons, 2001.

Buranen, Lisa, and Alice M. Roy, eds. *Perspectives on Plagiarism and Intellectual Property in a Postmodern World*. Albany, N.Y.: State University of New York Press, 1999.

Correa, Carlos Maria. *Intellectual Property Rights, the WTO and Developing Countries: The Trips Agreement and Policy Options*. New York: Zed Books, 2000.

Davis, Michael H., et al. *Intellectual Property: Patents, Trademarks, and Copyright in a Nutshell*. St. Paul, Minn.: West Group, 2000.

Decoo, Wilfried. *Crisis on Campus: Confronting Academic Misconduct*. Cambridge, Mass.: MIT Press, 2002.

Elias, Stephen, and Richard Stim. *Patent, Copyright & Trademark*. Berkeley, Calif.: Nolo Press, 2003.

Evans, Tonya Marie. *Literary Law Guide for Authors*. Philadelphia, Pa.: FYOS Entertainment, LLC, 2003.

Fishman, Stephen. *The Copyright Handbook: How to Protect & Use Written Works*. Berkeley, Calif.: Nolo Press, 2002.

———. *The Public Domain: How to Find and Use Copyright-Free Writings, Music, Art, & More*. Berkeley, Calif.: Nolo Press, 2001.

———. *Web Software Development: A Legal Guide*. Berkeley, Calif.: Nolo Press, 2002.

Glazier, Stephen C. *e-Patent Strategies for Software, e-Commerce, the Internet, Telecom Services, Financial Services, and Business Methods (with Case Studies and Forecasts)*. Washington, D.C.: LBI Institute, 2000.

Goldstein, Paul. *Copyright's Highway: From Gutenberg to the Celestial Jukebox*. Stanford, Calif.: Stanford University Press, 2003.

———. *International Intellectual Property: Cases and Materials*. New York: Foundation Press, 2001.

Jaffe, Adam B., and Manuel Trajtenberg. *Patents, Citations, and Innovations: A Window on the Knowledge Economy*. Cambridge, Mass.: MIT Press, 2002.

Jassin, Lloyd J., and Steven C. Schecter. *The Copyright Permission and Libel Handbook: A Step-By-Step Guide for Writers, Editors, and Publishers*. New York: John Wiley & Sons, 1998.

Keet, Ernest E. *Preventing Piracy: A Business Guide to Software Protection*. Reading, Mass.: Addison-Wesley Pub. Co., 1985.

Landes, William M., and Richard A. Posner. *The Economic Structure of Intellectual Property Law*. Cambridge, Mass.: Harvard University Press, 2003.

Lathrop, Ann, and Kathleen Foss. *Student Cheating and Plagiarism in the Internet Era: A Wake-Up Call*. Englewood, Colo.: Libraries Unlimited, 2000.

Lechter, Michael A., and Robert T. Kiyosaki. *Protecting Your #1 Asset: Creating Fortunes from Your Ideas: An Intellectual Property Handbook*. New York: Warner Books, 2001.

Lessig, Lawrence. *Code, and Other Laws of Cyberspace*. New York: Basic Books, 1999.

Lindey, Alexander. *Plagiarism and Originality*. Westport, Conn.: Greenwood Press, 1974.

Lindsey, Marc. *Copyright Law on Campus*. Pullman, Wash.: Washington State University Press, 2003.

Litman, Jessica. *Digital Copyright: Protecting Intellectual Property on the Internet*. Amherst, N.Y.: Prometheus Books, 2001.

Mallon, Thomas. *Stolen Words*. San Diego, Calif.: Harcourt, 2001.

Maskus, Keith E., and C. Fred Bergsten. *Intellectual Property Rights in the Global Economy*. Washington, D.C.: Institute for International Economics, 2000.

Megantz, Robert C. *Technology Management: Developing and Implementing Effective Licensing Programs*. New York: John Wiley & Sons, 2002.

Poltorak, Alexander, and Paul Lerner. *Essentials of Intellectual Property*. New York: John Wiley & Sons, 2002.

Pressman, David. *Patent It Yourself*. Berkeley, Calif.: Nolo Press, 2002.

Rawicz, Leonard, and Ralph C. Nash Jr. *Intellectual Property in Government Contracts: Computer Software, Information and Contract Remedies*. Chicago: Commerce Clearing House, 2001.

Razgaitis, Richard. *Valuation and Pricing of Technology-Based Intellectual Property*. New York: John Wiley & Sons, 2003.

Rivette, Kevin G., and David Kline. *Rembrandts in the Attic: Unlocking the Hidden Value of Patents*. Boston: Harvard Business School Press, 2000.

Smith, Gordon V., and Russell L. Parr. *Valuation of Intellectual Property and Intangible Assets*. New York: John Wiley & Sons, 2000.

Stobbs, Gregory A. *Software Patents*. Gaithersburg, Md.: Aspen Law & Business, 2000.

Sullivan, Patrick H. *Value-Driven Intellectual Capital: How to Convert Intangible Corporate Assets Into Market Value*. New York: John Wiley & Sons, 2000.

Thierer, Adam, and Wayne Crews, eds. *Copy Fights: The Future of Intellectual Property in the Information Age*. Washington, D.C.: Cato Institute, 2002.

Vaidhyanathan, Siva. *Copyrights and Copywrongs: The Rise of Intellectual Property and How It Threatens Creativity*. New York: New York University Press, 2003.

Web Sites

This section offers the reader a list of Web sites that can provide more extensive information on intellectual property, acquiring and protecting copyrights, patents, and trademarks, and organizations that grant permissions to copyrighted works. These Web sites also include links to other sites that may be of help or interest. Due to the nature of the Internet, the continued existence of a site is never guaranteed, but at the time of this book's publication, all of these Internet addresses were in operation.

United States Copyright Office
www.copyright.gov

Provides instructions and forms for obtaining copyrights.

United States Patent and Trademark Office
www.uspto.gov

Provides information on patents, trademarks, copyrights, domain names, and international intellectual property while also describing what can be patented and who may apply for patents. It also provides the fees and forms for acquiring a patent.

European Copyright User Platform
www.eblida.org/ecup

The latest information on European copyright developments.

Federal Communications Commission
www.fcc.gov

The official Web site of the FCC, which regulates interstate and international communications by radio, television, wire, satellite, and cable.

Government Printing Office Access
www.gpoaccess.gov

A service of the U.S. Government Printing Office, providing free electronic access to informative materials produced by the Federal Government.

World Intellectual Property Organization
www.wipo.org

The official Web site of the WIPO, an organization which strives to maintain respect for intellectual property worldwide and fights to gain cheaper, easier, and more secure protection for intellectual property.

American Society of Composers, Authors, and Publishers
www.ascap.com

An association for those in the music industry who strive to protect the rights of their copyrighted works. The site also explains how to become a member.

Authors Registry
www.authorsregistry.org

A nonprofit payment clearinghouse that works to ensure authors timely compensation from new-media sources that use their work.

Copyright Clearance Center
www.copyright.com

A Web site that grants permission to reproduce copyrighted materials.

Motion Picture Licensing Corporation
www.mplc.com

Established by major motion picture studios, this Web site grants umbrella licenses to non-profit groups, businesses, and government organizations to publicly show videos and DVDs.

Electronic Frontier Foundation (EFF)
www.eff.org

The official web site of the EFF, it works to protect basic rights online; to educate policymakers, the press, and the general public about civil liberties related to technology, as well as defend those liberties; and to provide current information about ongoing litigation in these areas, as well as a calendar of upcoming events.

RespectCopyrights.org
www.respectcopyrights.org

A Web site geared towards educating the public on the importance of respecting copyrights, mainly those for motion pictures. It attacks digital piracy and pleads against it.

Dal Libraries
www.library.dal.ca/how/detect.htm

Web site maintained by Dalhousie University in Halifax, Nova Scotia. Offers techniques on how to detect plagiarism among students. Also offers related Web sites that may be of assistance to educators.

Turnitin.com
www.turnitin.com

Designed for use by students and teachers to deter plagiarism. Includes research resources that define plagiarism and guide students in how to avoid plagiarizing in their papers.

Additional Periodical Articles with Abstracts

More information dealing with intellectual property and related subjects can be found in the following articles. Readers who require a more comprehensive selection are advised to consult *Readers' Guide to Periodical Literature, Readers' Guide Abstracts, Social Sciences Abstracts, General Science Abstracts, Humanities Abstracts,* and other H.W. Wilson publications.

Brainpower on the Balance Sheet. Adam Aston. *Business Week*, pp110–11 August 19–26, 2002.

Aston asserts that, in today's business environment, companies need a greater tolerance of uncertainty. He says they should be allowed to assign monetary values to such intangible assets as intellectual property, patents, brands, and customer lists, which can help investors make wiser decisions. Moreover, as the embodiment of ideas, intangibles are the drivers of growth in an information economy, but investors who read statements prepared under accounting principles generally accepted in the United States can only guess at their value or composition. Invisible assets that should be given dollar values are discussed.

Who Are the Electronic Learners? Why Should We Worry About Them? Frank W. Connolly. *Change*, v. 26 pp39–41 March/April 1994.

According to Connolly, the "virtual" communities made possible by computer networks can give students, teachers, and researchers access to vast resources, but they also open the campus to a world of outsiders, some of whom are demagogues and malcontents. This openness raises a host of issues, including plagiarism, harassment, and access, that universities and colleges must be prepared to address. The American Association for Higher Education's proposed Bill of Rights and Responsibilities for Electronic Learners is discussed.

Consumers, Digital Technology, and Copyrights. James Plummer. *Consumers' Research Magazine*, v. 85 pp34–5 September 2002.

Plummer recounts Hollywood's growing anxiety over the expansion of computer-processing power and the bandwidths of Web connections. As DVD recorders are dropping in price and consumers on peer-to-peer (P2P) file-trading networks have taken the next step and begun to download copyrighted video as well as audio, major media conglomerates are calling on Congress to codify a complicated Digital Rights Management scheme that would permit the studios to hack into the computers of unlawful file-trading consumers. They are also leaning on the Justice Department to prosecute traders of unauthorized copies of copyrighted material on P2P networks. The writer outlines the arguments put forth by Hollywood on this issue.

The Law & Economics of Intellectual Property. Richard A. Posner. *Daedalus*, v. 131 pp5–12 Spring 2002.

No field of law is in a greater uproar than intellectual property law, according to Posner. Legal disputes over intellectual property have exploded in recent years, facilitated inevitably by the rise of the information economy, which was built on intellectual property. Due to the fact that intellectual property is America's largest export, its importance is considerable, and this is one of the major factors that lie behind the seemingly relentless expansion of modern IP laws. This expansion is illustrated by the repeated enlargement of the copyright term in recent years to the point where it is almost perpetual, and by the new "business method" patents. Posner explains that these developments have created the potential for inventors of new business approaches to obtain enormous monopoly power and develop a reward greatly in excess of the cost of the invention.

We All Pay for Internet Plagiarism. Ellen Laird. *The Education Digest*, v. 67 pp56–9 November 2001.

Laird discusses the growing problem of plagiarism and how students take information from the Internet, regardless of whether they need it or even know what it means. In most cases, Internet cheating is hard to spot and texts that students download from the Internet are written by other students. The author also discusses the limitless sources for researched writing published online and how these resources can be acquired by most students with a college I.D. through electronic databases. These sources on a "works cited" page are inconspicuous and make the plagiarism even more convincing. This kind of plagiarism may soon drive course content and shape reading lists.

Copyrights and Wrongs. Colleen Bonniol and Bob Bonniol. *Entertainment Design*, v. 37 pp40 March 2003.

The writers offer advice for projection designers on navigating the contentious world of intellectual property rights.

Copyrights and Wrongs, Part 2. Colleen Bonniol and Bob Bonniol. *Entertainment Design*, v. 37 pp28–9 April 2003.

This article details the debate in artistic, intellectual, and legal circles about what defines the idea of intellectual property and copyright. The authors look at the most recent interpretation of intellectual property by the U.S. Supreme Court, which upheld the Sonny Bono Copyright Extension Act. Under this act many copyrights held by major media companies will now extend for 95 years, with individual copyrights extending for the life of the author/creator plus 70 years. The authors maintain that the extension is designed to ensure the stability of big corporate revenue streams, and that it has now shrunk the available pool of public-domain and pending public-domain candidates. The writers advise designers on how to protecting themselves from copyright litigation.

Mine Games. Eric W. Pfeiffer. *Forbes*, v. 169 pp60–2 June 24, 2002.

Eric W. Pfeiffer examines British Telecommunications' decision to transfer over 14,000 of its global patents to ipValue Management, a company based in Mountain View, California. In exchange for a share of future revenues, start-up ipValue has agreed to assess which patents are valuable enough to be sold or licensed. Formed to help companies manage their patents and other intellectual property, ipValue is backed by Goldman Sachs and the Boston Consulting Group and led by Joe Zier, the former head of KPMG's intellectual-property practice. The decision by such powerhouses to move into a field dominated by boilerplate patent attorneys is a sign, Pfeiffer believes, that after years of unfulfilled promises, the business of managing intellectual property could be ripe for new growth and moneymaking.

Fighting Cyberplagiarism. Brian C. Smith. *Library Journal*, pp22–3 Summer 2003.

Smith provides six strategies that educators and librarians can employ to address the problem of Internet plagiarism.

Copyright Monopolies. Andrew L. Shapiro. *The Nation*, v. 276 pp6–7 February 17, 2003.

Andrew L. Shapiro explores Big Media's victory in another round of the escalating copyright war. The Supreme Court recently upheld the 1998 Copyright Term Extension Act (known as the Sonny Bono Act), which extends new and existing copyright terms by 20 years—to life plus 70 years for individuals and to 95 years for corporations. The case before it, *Eldred v. Ashcroft*, gave the Supreme Court a chance to correct the balance between copyright and free speech and to reaffirm that copyright must serve the public interest. Shapiro argues that the Court's 7–2 ruling against doing so is a blow to consumer rights and free speech and sets terrible precedents.

When It Raines . . . Eric Alterman. *The Nation*, v. 276 pp10+ June 30, 2003.

The writer discusses the media's reaction to the scandal caused by *New York Times* journalist Jayson Blair, which resulted in the resignation of Howell Raines and Gerald Boyd, the two top editors of the paper.

Righting Copywrongs. James Surowiecki. *The New Yorker*, v. 77 pp27 January 21, 2002.

James Surowiecki examines the passage by Congress of the so-called Sonny Bono Act, which extended all copyrights for an additional 20 years. The act resulted from some aggressive lobbying and well-targeted campaign contributions from Disney and others, acknowledges Surowiecki. He also looks at the opposition, headed by Lawrence Lessig, then a law professor at Harvard and now at Stanford, who helped orchestrate a lawsuit to challenge the act's constitutionality. Lessig believes that the act is not merely another instance of favoritism but is part of a disastrous trend toward what might be termed property-rights fundamentalism. He believes that this trend could destroy the Internet and plunge society into a cultural dark age.

Software Bullet Is Sought to Kill Musical Piracy. Andrew Ross Sorkin. *New York Times* (Late New York Edition), ppA1+ May 4, 2003.

Sorkin writes that, according to industry executives, many of the world's largest record companies, in the face of rampant online piracy, are quietly financing the development and testing of software programs that would sabotage the computers and Internet connections of persons who download pirated music. He discusses this new phenomenon and its effect on would-be pirates.

Studios Using Digital Armor to Fight Piracy. Amy Harmon. *New York Times* (Late New York Edition), pp1+ January 5, 2003.

Amy Harmon focuses on Hollywood's newly imposed restrictions on digital movies, television, and music after years of battling online piracy in court.

Cheat Wave. Richard Jerome. *People*, v. 57 pp83–4 June 17, 2002.

Jerome looks at the story of Christine Pelton, a biology teacher at Piper High School in Piper, Kansas, who told 28 of her students who had plagiarized that she planned to give them no credit for an assignment that was to count for half of that semester's grade. When parents rose up in protest, the school board ruled that the project would count for only 30 percent of the grade. This article recounts the resignation of Pelton and of the nine fellow teachers—including the principal and vice principal—who joined her in protest.

Reading the Future. Rebecca Day. *Popular Mechanics*, v. 178 pp82–5 April 2001.

Rebecca Day provides an overview of electronic books, or e-book technology. She considers 2001 the dawn of a new age in technology, with more advanced digital readers coming to market, more tech-savvy customers emerging, encryption protection and digital copyrights for authors and publishers in development, and the publication of a more compelling selection of e-book titles. She also discusses a number of new e-book reading devices.

Prying Eyes Invade Your CDs. Stephen A. Booth. *Popular Science*, v. 259 pp39 November 2001.

Booth focuses on major record labels and the new tests they're conducting to prevent the pirating of CDs. Today, copying recorded music via PCs and CD burners is a common method of pirating recordings, but this process was not foreseen when the Audio Home Recording Act was first passed. To combat this growing problem, five major record labels are testing new electronic technologies aimed at protecting copyrights. Hackers, however, have already begun a counterattack, with one German group claiming to have beaten Sony's key2audio. Booth looks at these new technologies and what they could mean for the music industry.

Cheater, Cheater . . . Kelley R. Taylor. *Principal Leadership*, v. 3 pp74–7 April 2003.

Taylor provides advice to educators on combating plagiarism and cheating. The writer urges educators to appreciate the "big picture"; acquire and share knowledge about intellectual property rules; develop and implement clear, acknowledged policies; set forth unambiguous penalties and enforce them consistently; employ practical strategies to combat the problem; and remember due process.

Let's Put the Heat on Campus Cheats. Stephen Barr. *Reader's Digest*, v. 156 pp108–13 May 2000.

Barr examines the increase in plagiarism, unauthorized collaboration on assignments, and cheating on tests reported by numerous colleges and universities over the past few years. Research by a Rutgers University professor at 31 schools over the past 10 years shows that almost 70 percent of students admit to cheating at some time during college. Barr explains that the Internet has made it easier than ever to cheat, with Web sites facilitating the exchange of papers between students and the downloading of ready-made essays on a range of topics. He also looks at how an increasing number of third-level institutions are reintroducing the honor code in an attempt to address the problem and how new honors programs have established procedures for dealing with students who are caught cheating.

IP Policies and Serving the Public. Roger N. Beachy. *Science*, v. 299 pp473 January 24, 2003.

With scientific discoveries leading to the development of new drugs, crops, and foods, universities have been more aggressive than expected in pursuing the protection of inventions. According to Beachy, current intellectual-property policies and the reluctance of companies to license valuable discoveries make it difficult to apply new technologies to address problems in developing countries, especially when these countries lack policies for defining IP rights or procedures for premarket approval. He believes that academic research institutions should make the results of research available to developing countries and that scientists should be encouraged to do research targeted to the public good, including projects that will benefit developing countries.

IP Rights—And Wrongs. Gary Stix. *Scientific American*, v. 286 pp38 May 2002.

Stix looks at the role of federal investigators in examining whether broad patent and copyright protection inhibits competition. He discusses the new trend which has forced policy makers in Washington, D.C., to question whether intellectual property rights are too strong and are hindering competition in software and other technology markets. He also examines the hearings initiated by the Federal Trade Commission and the Department of Justice to determine whether some patents inhibit innovation and whether a proliferation of patents influences competition.

Razing the Tollbooths. Gary Stix. *Scientific American*, v. 288 pp37 April 2003.

Stix examines the ongoing debate in the intellectual-property community over the Bayh-Dole Act, a 1980 law that encourages the patenting of academic research and the exclusive licensing of those patents to industry. While the law has caused a 14-fold increase in patents awarded to universities, some have recently contended that the development of new biotechnologies has been hindered by extending patent coverage beyond actual products to basic research findings. In this article, Stix presents the argument that DNA sequences, protein structures, and disease pathways should, in many cases, function as a general knowledge base that can be used freely by everyone.

Some Rights Reserved. Gary Stix. *Scientific American*, v. 288 pp46 March 2003.

The nonprofit Creative Commons Web site, initiated by Lawrence Lessig and other cyber-activists, is the focus of Stix's article. The site advocates providing licenses that enable copyrighted works to be shared more easily. Stix describes the site's online questionnaire, which allows creators to customize a license and copyright their work while stipulating that only some rights are reserved. He looks at how this Web site enables public work to be shared and how a commons for creative exchange can become a reality in cyberspace.

Sounding Board. *Smart Computing*, v. 14 pp108 February 2003.

In this article, a number of computer-industry professionals comment on the growing popularity of software that requires user "activation" in order to run.

Eyes Wide Shut. Laura Evenson. *Sound & Vision*, v. 68 pp40 January 2003.

Evenson examines MovieMask, a censoring software from Trilogy Studios used to edit objectionable content from DVDs. She describes how it works and suggests that MovieMask may be an effective way to sanitize almost any movie with a PG or R rating. Nevertheless, it has already raised many objections from Hollywood directors, who argue that it violates copyrights and usurps their artistic control.

Information Wants a Fee. Robert Buderi. *Technology Review*, v. 105 pp9 November 2002.

Buderi contends that the mantra of the Internet age—"information wants to be free"—should be "information wants a fee." He argues that too many people have extended the meaning of free from "let loose" to "let loose without charge," a condition which cannot last. The challenge, Buderi explains, will be to find the right balance of fair use and fair compensation, so that digital music and movies will have the kind of protection long enjoyed by other types of information and consumers will pay for value received.

Science Goes Medieval. Seth Shulman. *Technology Review*, v. 105 pp101 June 2002.

Shulman examines a survey of 1,240 geneticists at 100 universities which shows that 73 percent believe that the withholding of data among their colleagues is hampering progress in their field. The findings, compiled by a doctor at Massachusetts General Hospital, are particularly remarkable, according to Shulman, because the robust exchange of information is a central principle in science, where knowledge grows by being shared.

Plagiarism Is Just a Mouseclick Away. Chris Bunting. *The Times Higher Education Supplement*, pp24 December 13, 2002.

Bunting discusses the problem of cheating in Great Britain. Anecdotal reports suggest that students use text messaging to cheat during examinations, although there is little hard evidence to support the assertion that cheating on exams is on the rise. However, a combination of students' lax attitudes and new technology may be causing increased cheating in assessed course work with unattributed material being lifted from the Internet in instances of "mouseclick" plagiarism.

The Day the Music (Almost) Died. Paul Sloan and James Lardner. *U.S. News & World Report*, v. 129 pp54 August 7, 2000.

Sloan and Lardner explain the decision of federal district judge Marilyn Patel, who found the online music-swapping site Napster guilty of piracy and copyright infringement. Napster's popularity, the writers say, has told the music industry that it must quickly formulate legitimate methods of online distribution that approximate Napster's ease of use in order to survive in a high-tech society. The writers also discuss further implications of the judgment for the recording industry.

This Man Vs. Mickey Mouse. Craig Cox. *Utne*, pp83 January/February 2003.

Stanford law professor Lawrence Lessig's appearance before the Supreme Court in October 2002 to discuss copyright on the Internet is the subject of Cox's article. Cox looks at the recent extension of copyright protection from 75 to 95 years, which, according to Lessig, is an example of massive corporations striving to foil the development of the Internet as the grand digital commons of shared information. Opponents like Lessig also contend that the copyright extensions offered by the act violate the Constitution's intention of providing only "limited" copyright protection as a way of promoting "the progress of science and useful arts." Cox reviews these issues and the controversy surrounding the new law.

Index